KINAUVIT?

KINAUVIT?

What's Your Name?

THE ESKIMO DISC SYSTEM
AND A DAUGHTER'S SEARCH
FOR HER GRANDMOTHER

Dr. Norma Dunning

Douglas & McIntyre

DOUGLAS AND MCINTYRE (2013) LTD.
P.O. Box 219, Madeira Park, BC, V0N 2H0
www.douglas-mcintyre.com

EDITED by Peter Midgley
INDEXED by Martin Gavin
DUST JACKET DESIGN by Dwayne Dobson
TEXT DESIGN by Libris Simas Ferraz / Onça Design
PRINTED AND BOUND in Canada

DOUGLAS AND MCINTYRE acknowledges the support of the Canada Council for the Arts, the Government of Canada, and the Province of British Columbia through the BC Arts Council.

LIBRARY AND ARCHIVES CANADA CATALOGUING IN PUBLICATION
Title: Kinauvit? = What's your name? : the Eskimo disc system and a
    daughter's search for her grandmother / Dr. Norma Dunning.
Other titles: What's your name?
Names: Dunning, Norma, author.
Description: Includes bibliographical references and index.
Identifiers: Canadiana (print) 20220241333 | Canadiana (ebook)
    20220241341 | ISBN 9781771623391 (hardcover) | ISBN
    9781771623407 (EPUB)
Subjects: LCSH: Inuit—Canada—History. | LCSH: Inuit—Canada—
    Government relations. | LCSH: Inuit—Legal status, laws,
    etc.—Canada.
Classification: LCC E99.E7 D86 2022 | DDC 971.004/971—dc23

This work is dedicated to all Inuit Canadians past, present, and future. Stand tall and always remember that we are more than a number.

Contents

Acknowledgements

I would like to acknowledge all the Inuit who freely and openly interviewed for this work: Susan Aglukark, Lucie Idlout, Zebedee Nungak, Martha Hatkaitok, David Serkoak, and Alan Voisey. Your voices enriched and gave reality to my work. Ma'na.

I would like to thank Dr Nathalie Kermoal, Dr Brendan Hokowhitu and Dr Sourayan Mookerjea, who each supported the research and writing of this work as a Master of Arts thesis through the Faculty of Native Studies at the University of Alberta, Edmonton.

My thanks to my agent Stephanie Sinclair, who saw value in this work. Thank you to all the folks at D&M—Anna and Claire, and early edits by Shari Narine. You each put hours into making things come together.

My special thanks to Peter Midgley, editor extraordinaire, who saw more than I could when transitioning a scholarly work into a personal story of searching and hoping and realizing some stones must remain unturned.

Ma'na to my dear, dear mom Theresa Dunning—this book exists because of you. Your voice kept this research going, even on the days when I didn't want to. I love you forever, Mom. xoxoxo

#

(Family)

"Mom, what are we?"

I remember that Saturday afternoon when I walked into the kitchen of our military base duplex. It was the kind of Saturday that only the prairies can give. Not one bit of a breeze anywhere. The heat penetrating my eight-year-old body making me feel like I was a human magnifying glass. I was so loaded with the swelter of summer that I could have burned footprints into the well-worn path between the playground and my house.

The aroma of cooking oil was singing against the kitchen walls while the deep fryer bubbled a happy tune on the counter. Deep fryers can trigger the hunger inside of all of us. Mom had her back to me and was peeling potatoes. She was making home fries. A Saturday supper favourite.

I asked my question a second time and my mom spun around with a paring knife in one hand and a potato balanced in the palm of her other hand. She bent toward me and asked, "Who wants to know?"

I felt like I had said a bad word. I had said the wrong thing. I had done something that I would have to take into the church confessional tomorrow. She repeated her question one more time, "Who wants to know?"

"I do," I said in an almost-whisper. I was confused. It was a simple question. I wasn't understanding why she had answered my question with a question.

"You?" Mom knew better. She had a way of seeing through my sweaty round self. She always knew when I was making things up.

"All the kids at the playground were saying what they are and then they asked me, and I said, 'I don't know,' and they all laughed at me."

"And what are they?"

"They're Swedish and Italian and German and one boy has an uncle who's a real-life pirate!"

She let loose a low giggle. "Well Norma, you tell people this: Tell them you're French! You were born in Quebec and that's all they need to know!"

Mom turned back to the counter and her skilled hands went back to slicing the potato. The paring knife looked like an extra finger. It was a part of her. Cutting and scraping, working with knives and blades was familiar. Something she was born into.

I grew up in a house with tight rules and strict ways of behaving. We were a family that never spoke of the past, only the present. Never yesterday. Our lives were precision-filled routines. I never once displayed any real emotions and always did as ordered. Never the unexpected.

The next time I was at the playground I proudly told the other little kids that I was French. It never once entered my head that I was anything else but French, even with the last name of Dunning.

When I said that I was French no one questioned my dark eyes or hair or high cheek bones. No one asked for any further details and because no one else asked, I didn't either. I went along well into my teens feeling fairly secure in telling other people that I was born in Quebec. My mom was fluent in French, and I took French classes, therefore I was definitely French. I could put all of that information out into the world but inside of me sat an unease.

It was the unease of knowing that there was a secret humming inside of my family. It was growing older and watching how my parents operated in the world. How our lives revolved around the seasons of each year. How fall was hunting and plucking geese and seeing hide-less moose meat dangling in cold garages. How winter was being outside and playing for hours and hours in the snow and never learning how to stop on my ice skates. I spent year after year crashing into outdoor rink boards. Spring bore summer and summer was camping and being barefoot and days when the tight restrictions of time would loosen.

Summer was riding in the old station wagon for hours and hours and finally stopping to camp and build a fire and run with the feeling of a freed stallion. Summer was playing Indian rubber with a bat and a small hard black ball that left bruises everywhere on our bodies because each of my brothers and sisters wanted to win at a game that was without rules.

Summer was when our lives were released from the routine of Dad's drinking and beating Mom and the fear of Friday nights. Summer brought a calmness over all of us, but that sense of unease lingered inside of me. Not knowing what we were mixed itself up with trying to understand the small things that happened. I was always trying to understand why we were treated the way we were by some relatives. The secret inside of my family hummed and grew taller with me as things happened with Dad's family that I never understood.

Things like when we visited my dad's side of the family. Why was our trailer always set up at the farthest spot from the farmhouse? Why did his sisters, my aunts, make us wash our hands over and over again? Why were we never allowed into their houses except for meals? Was it because our eyes and hair colour didn't match their blue eyes and strawberry blonde hair? Were we really all that different?

In truth, we were. We were not a Presbyterian family. We were not farm people. We were not people who worked and lived on the same parcel of land year after year and decade after decade.

We were a military family who moved every other year to yet another obscure posting. We lived on small bases in government-supplied housing and went to school on base. We were a group of untethered people who took solace in the confines of military life. The security of the curfew siren at 9 p.m. that sent us all home. We grew up around the hierarchy of military existence, meaning that my father who was a sergeant sat near the bottom of the military totem pole. It was a life where you were treated by others based on your father's rank and where officers' kids got away with everything.

By the time I finished high school I had sat through eight different schools in three different provincial education systems. Life was always about our next transfer. Every other summer my mom would bring me a small box and say, "Put your favourite things in here for the moving men." I was allowed to keep only what I could carry, and I would write "Norma's" on the cardboard flap.

We lived in Winnipeg when I was in Grade 10. It was the first city I had ever lived in. The sound of constant traffic on Corydon Avenue was unbearable. I had to learn how to take public transport. I had to learn how to operate like a city kid and not the small military-base person that I had grown up as. Winnipeg brought me one thing that I had never had before. Winnipeg brought me northern cousins and my one auntie—one of my mom's sisters who was from Churchill and who would visit when she was in town.

My Auntie Frances was the one who let the word "Inuit" loose into the air. She was talking to my mom about "the convent" they had attended for their schooling. The afternoon she dared to speak that word was the first day I heard Mom "sh" her. "Don't talk about that," Mom said. The convent was not a topic for discussion.

The unease that lay inside of me started to stir. Now two new things had come into play: "Inuit" and "the convent." Auntie would come and go during our one year in Winnipeg and I learned to stay close to her when she was in town. Maybe she would start to fill up the holes that my unease contained. Maybe I would get more information from her.

I did. The stories never had a beginning or an ending. The stories were tiny sentences that arrived from nowhere like an unexpected guest who walks into your house, sits down in your favourite chair and leaves moments later. I started to hear the name Cecil "Husky" Harris and along with his name, northern people started appearing on our doorstep. Northern people who had lived in Churchill with my parents during the first ten years of their marriage. Northern people who were former trappers. They were people who were not white.

A part of my own unease lay in the fact that I knew I wasn't white. I knew that I wasn't French. I knew that I didn't look like my dad's family. I knew that the words "Inuit" or "the convent" were words that were never allowed to be spoken or set free from my mouth. I also knew that my mom would never answer any questions that I had.

I never asked, "Mom, what are we?" again but I kept working at putting together the pieces of me. The pieces of that puzzle would come to me when I started to read about the history of Churchill. When I looked at pictures of Inuit and then looked in the mirror searching for similarities. Who was I in the world? I had to know.

Life tumbled past me and I worked various jobs that I had no real interest in. All four of my sons arrived within eight years. I was a busy mom. Working and raising the boys who made my every day worth every breath that I took. I was so in love with each of them.

I started to think about how they should know who and what they are. My mother had passed away by the time I ignited my research. I was trying to understand what being Inuit meant. I did the most daring thing I had ever done. I declared my Inuitness by applying to the Nunavut beneficiary program requesting enrolment on the Inuit Enrolment List. Being on that list would entitle me to benefit from the Nunavut Land Claims Agreement (NLCA) for as long as I was alive.

My heart rate picked up a bit and the tension spread across my shoulders as I fed my application and the applications of my sons into the fax machine one early work morning in 2001. One of my brothers had applied for and received Nunavut beneficiary status and had encouraged me to apply. He had been encouraged to apply by one of our northern cousins. He had received beneficiary status and told me about the process.

I was beginning to put into place a legal definition of who I was and who my sons were. It was finally cementing in and filling up the hole of unease that had followed me around for the first forty years of my life. It was fulfilling a sense of belonging. I was awakening a sense of kinship. I was discovering a different sense of family.

Applying for Nunavut beneficiary status was asking for acceptance from my own Inuit. I was nervous about that. If I were to secure Nunavut beneficiary status it would mean that I would have acceptance from Nunangat Inuit, those who live in what is my land claims area and my ancestral homeland of Nunavut.

My sons and I have always lived south of sixty. It would mean that I could prove that I was what I said I was. My boys could do the same. That was important. The pieces of paper being faxed to Nunavut would solidify my existence as an Inuk woman.

I regret that my mom never spoke openly about her own Inuitness or her upbringing. It took me decades to recognize that her upbringing was painfilled. Inside of the decades since being a Grade 10 kid in Winnipeg, I had learned that "the convent" was a residential school located outside of Winnipeg. I learned of the abusive treatment that she and her two sisters had survived through the stories my one auntie told and my own research. I learned that she and her sisters were little Inuit girls who grew up without any understanding of what love is. No child learned that inside of a residential school. How can someone give something that they have no concept of? They never heard the words "I love you" or felt the comfort and security that a hug can bring. Soft touches and words of care were never given freely to them, and they did not give them freely to us.

What I learned most was to not hold anything from my childhood against my mom. I do not say that with pity or as an act of absolution toward my good mom. I say this because as adults we must step back and understand our parents as individuals. I learned that when my mom spoke of her younger years she started with her marriage to my dad. Her twenty-two years before him did not exist.

It was during that one year in Winnipeg that I approached her about "the convent." It was the only time we ever spoke of it. My father was away that year moving heavy equipment into the North as part of a military assignment. While he was away, I had taken to riding the city bus home for lunch. It was the only time that my mom and I were completely alone. We would eat her good food and we would sit with our cups of tea for a few minutes before I took public transit back to the high school that I hated.

I wanted to know more about her childhood. I remember the sense of nervous anticipation that one noon hour. Mom was talking about her early years of marriage in Churchill. She was telling stories of babysitting for my auntie, and we were laughing. I asked her if she knew how to cook when she married my dad. She laughed about all the food that she had burned. I was fortunate because I was number five out of six children. By the time I was born my mother truly was an amazing cook.

I recall thinking that if I didn't ask her about "the convent" that day I would never have the guts to ask her again. I blurted out my question: "Mom, what was the convent like?" Silence fell between us. She looked away. Her response consisted of five words, "It was very, very hard." Five words that summed up her younger years before she married a military man and celebrated fifty-two wedding anniversaries with him. It took me a few decades to fill in that one sentence with an understanding of why Theresa Marie Harris never spoke of "the convent" and why we were raised with all the tight rules and a routine that never changed.

It also took me a few decades to figure out her alcoholism and her sudden fits of anger that manifested in sharp slaps across my face when I least expected it. Her words of loathing would arrive out of nowhere, slicing my soul in half. Her extreme behaviours mirrored her upbringing. Inside of that upbringing was a sense of Indigenous shame. Inside of her behaviour lay the story of her youth and how she and her two sisters survived "the convent." Words that were never spoken instead became strong actions of aggression and assault in her early motherhood years.

I began to understand why she never identified or allowed her children to identify as Inuit. I loved my mom with a kind heart because I began to realize that kindness was not often extended toward her. I began to understand that hiding her Indigeneity was an easier path for her to take. She wanted her own children to not have to deal with being Inuit in Canada and what that meant if you lived outside of the tundra. I began to see how and why it was hard for her to say, "I love you," and how and why it was easier to drink gallons and gallons of Kelowna red wine. I began to understand why she had told me to tell others that I was French.

Through my Auntie Frances and the family I had met in Winnipeg, I had come full circle, and was now applying to officially re-establish my connection to my ancestral land. My mom died of cancer in 1999 and here I was in 2001 filling a fax machine with paperwork and hoping that my boss wouldn't come in early and catch me. Here I was trying to claim something that Mom never did—Nunavut beneficiary status. I will always say that my mom knew what she was and did not need to carry a beneficiary card to prove it. She raised us without identifying what we were. Some forms of protection lie inside of silence. It is not wrong to let six children travel separate paths of self-discovery. The application sliding through the fax machine was one of the first steps I took on that path.

Inuit Canadians having beneficiary status is not the same as being Status First Nation or an accepted member of a Métis community. Federal Court Judge Sébastien Grammond, whose early PhD work examined the legal recognition of Indigenous identity, summed up Inuit beneficiary status as,

> The fact that the Inuit have never been governed
> by the Indian Act and have no prior experience of
> excluding women who "married out" which may
> explain why it has been possible to recognize their
> total autonomy in membership matters...The system
> in Nunavut...according to certain local committee
> members [states] a person is an Inuk if one of his

or her parents are Inuit. There is no minimal blood
quantum. Marriage does not confer Inuit status.
There are no circumstances under which a person
can cease to be Inuk, although an Inuk may ask to
be removed from the enrolment list.[1]

From a legal standpoint that paragraph is saying Inuit
are not First Nations nor are First Nations, Inuit. However,
in mainstream Canada, First Nations and Inuit are often
blended together in the same cooking pot along with the
entire Métis population. Mainstream will often see all
Indigenous Canadians as one and the same when in truth we
are each distinct and unique from one another. The Indian
Act governs Status First Nations, meaning that Métis and
Inuit are not included under the Indian Act. To the best of
my knowledge, Canada is the only country in the world that
still keeps an act that legislates all First Nation life.

Within the Indian Act there are countless amendments.
One is directed at Status First Nations women who dared to
fall in love with someone who was not a Status First Nations
male. A woman's standing as a member of a Status First
Nation was stripped from her and she was forced to live off
of her reserve. She could not participate in ceremony or cele-
brations. She was not able to be buried on her home reserve
and, above all, the federal government's fiduciary obliga-
tions toward her and her children were removed. A harsh

---

1   Grammond, *Identity Captured by Law*, 134.

outcome for not loving the right person as defined by the federal government. Because they do not fall under the Indian Act, Inuit do not have these same legalities attached to their identity. If an Inuk marries a non-Inuit person, that person does not become an Inuk and marriage does not erase an Inuk's ancestry.

Under the regulations of the NLCA, Inuit have full control of land claims membership without any federal government intervention. Inuit communities control who is accepted as members of their land claims agreements. There is no clause stating a removal of status for loving and marrying someone who is not Inuit. However, marrying a man or woman who is not an Inuk does not suddenly make that person an Inuk; this is very different from the Indian Act. Status First Nations males were always able to marry whomever they wanted, and that automatically gave that woman and all future children First Nations status.

The way the federal government has ruled over the lives of Status First Nations is in effect a way of enforcing blood quantum. Inuit do not have any conditions on having to be half or one-quarter or one-third Inuk to be accepted as a beneficiary. All that is required is that one parent, male or female, is an Inuk and an application can be put forward based on that alone. The idea of blood quantum is Eurocentric-based. It is not how Indigenous Canadians look at or measure one another. This is another concept that is difficult for the mainstream to accept. The way Indigenous Canadians view one another is not a matter of producing a government-issued card stating an "R" number for First Nations or "N" number for Inuit or a membership card for Métis.

What has happened to Inuit who reside in the south is that many younger Inuit do not make application into our ancestral home territory because they think that living in the south disqualifies them. Where you are currently living is not a part of the membership application and it saddens me that younger Inuit think that they are not Inuit because they have never been to or lived in the North of Canada. They have fallen into the thinking of non-Inuit. The ones who measure us by half or a quarter and think that we are not real because we live an everyday modern life outside of the North. I have learned over time to encourage all young Indigenous peoples to apply for First Nations status, Inuit beneficiary, and Métis community cards. I advise them to stop qualifying themselves as Indigenous to those who say they do not look or act it. Instead, I tell them, calmly look at the person who is telling them that their skin, hair, and eyes are not the right colour and ask that person, "Why do you think that?"

What this does is not only bring the power within the conversation back to Indigenous People, but those five words make the person who is telling them, "You don't look it," to examine their own colonial constructs and understandings. That small question of "why" places them in the position of trying to understand their own thinking. I always remind my students to never raise their voice as an Inuk. Never cause harm or heartache. Only look at that person and ask, "Why do you think that?" It is a form of quiet resistance. It is a form of decolonization. It is a way to begin a good relationship with an exchange of honest information. That is who Inuit are: kind people, open people, and people of good intent no matter where we are living.

Who and what we are on paper does not show the essence of being Inuit. Through the Nunavut Land Claims Agreement that was signed in 1993, the difference between who Inuit are on paper and who they are within themselves now lies in the location of an Inuk body. Those Inuit who live beyond the tundra are not included nor entitled to the same benefits as those Inuit who live within Nunavut. Inuit negotiators and the government of the day may have made this an intentional plan of action, resulting in Inuit residing in the south being left off the Inuit Enrolment List and those Inuit who stay in Nunavut, leery of leaving.

The Nunavut Land Claims Agreement was the outcome of a twenty-year process. According to the plain English guide to the agreement, Tukisittiarniqsaujumaviit? is an Inuktitut word that means "Would you like to have a better understanding?" It is also the title of the guide to the Nunavut Land Claims Agreement:[2]

An Inuk who is on the Inuit Enrolment list will benefit from the agreement. Another word for a person in

---

2   NTI, *Tukisittiarniqsaujumaviit*, 69.

this position is beneficiary. Inuit will decide who will be a beneficiary. Each community will choose who will have his or her name added to the enrolment list, using the rules set out in this Article (35). These say an eligible person:

· Is alive
· Is a Canadian citizen
· Is an Inuk according to Inuit custom
· Thinks of herself or himself as an Inuk
· Is associated with Nunavut, and
· Is not enrolled in any other Canadian land claims agreement at the same time.

Simply put, a beneficiary is an Inuit person who has ancestral ties to Nunavut and is recognized and remembered solely through family connections by community Elders and other community members. A beneficiary is then able to access various socio-economic benefits that are part of the government agreement pertaining to health and education. Note that the definition does not include a geographical positioning of an Inuk body and does not quantify who or what the ancestry of the person is.

It all appeared uncomplicated and straightforward. How could my sons and I not qualify for Nunavut beneficiary status based on the simple requirements and questions on the application form? I told myself to not worry about the application. Instead, I watched the paperwork slide onto the back tray of the fax machine. I reminded myself that I had done something of importance. I was finally filling up The Hole of Identity Unease. I was finally going to be able to confidently state what I am. A part of me yearned for that playground of long ago and wishing for those same small kids to ask again, "What are you?" My sons and I would stand at the bottom of that twirly slide and shout with pride and enthusiasm, "We're Inuit!"

tukihivit

(Understand... do you?)

Waiting for something is never fun. Days drip past us when we are waiting. Time slows to a near standstill. I had faxed and snail-mailed all of our paperwork North three months ago and still not one word from anyone. I didn't want to call them. I didn't want to appear pushy or rude. I kept telling myself that I could just keep waiting. But I couldn't. After watching ninety days slide past me on the calendar, I decided to call up North. I had a right to know, and calling was better than sending off a cold email. I would know immediately instead of another possible long wait for someone to hit reply.

I was nervous but I followed through and dialled out to the enrolment office. The voice that answered spoke in Inuktitut first and English second. I nervously explained in English who I was and that I wished to know the status of my sons' and my own application for enrolment. The woman who answered said she'd be right back. I wasn't put on hold. I could hear the shuffling of papers. I could hear a radio talking in Inuktitut as I waited. Those three minutes felt like forever and finally the woman asked an unexpected question: "What was your disc number?"

I was stunned. I didn't expect that question. I told the Inuk worker that I never had a disc number. Her response, "Well what was your mother's disc number?" Again I was shocked, and answered that my mom never had a disc. I heard small note of frustration in her voice when she said quietly, "Well, if either of you had one this would be much faster to process." I felt like I was being mildly scolded. I could not issue the automatic, "I'm sorry," that all Canadians say to excuse themselves in an awkward situation. The worker's final question was to ask if I had a copy of my mom's birth certificate. My answer was a quiet, "No."

That was the one question that I could answer with confidence. I knew my mom never had a birth certificate. I had found a document inside an old black Bible that had belonged to my dad's mother. It was a request for a search on my mom's birth date and year. The form was from the Department of Health and Public Welfare in the province of Manitoba. It was received on January 15, 1958, almost a year before I was born. It is addressed to Mrs. A.E. Dunning. It states: *Re: Birth of Therese Marie Harris: No record of this birth found in the years 1925, 1926, 1927 at Churchill, Manitoba.* The document also shows it cost fifty cents to have this information issued to her.

I had no government-issued proof of my Inuitness because, unlike my two older brothers and two older sisters, I had not been born in Churchill. I was without a document that proved a land claims area location. I was dumbstruck as I sat on the other end of the phone. All of the thoughts of proof of Inuit ancestry were swirling around me as I sat there with my mouth hanging open.

The worker then explained it was coming up to winter feast time and the office would be closed for a good while. I could check back in a month. I hung up the phone and sat in a puddle of confusion. A disc number? I knew what the worker had meant. I was aware of the disc system, but that system had shut down more than thirty years ago. The application did not ask for a disc number. Why in hell would I need a disc number? How did that number make an enrolment application process faster? I took out a piece of paper and started to write down what I did know. A pro and con list of Inuit ancestry, a physical rendering of what I knew so far. I could only write two lines.

Grandfather: Cecil "Husky" Harris—HBC factor, Poorfish Lake, died in Churchill, 1940, had three Inuit wives.
Names of his wives: (1) Angaviadniak—Padlei Inuit. The other two: unknown?

That's all I had for information. Two small lines of near nothing. I needed to find out more. I needed to start searching. I needed to hunt down my anaanatsiaq (grandmother) Angaviadniak's disc number. If I could provide her disc number then I would secure my evidence of being Eskimo.

A sense of panic sat inside my stomach. I had so very much work to do. The search for my grandmother's disc number became something of incredible importance to me. Something that would matter on an application. Something that would make her "real" to the governments of Canada and Nunavut. If I could find her number, I would be "real" too.

A disc number from an unseen and unknown grandmother carried as much importance to me today as it may have done to her so long ago. She had to be on a disc list. She had to be out there somewhere. All I had to do was find her. All I had to do was understand this part of her life. A life that I wanted proof of. A woman whose blood runs inside and alongside of mine and my mother's drove my desire to understand what the Eskimo Identification Canada system was.

The system obviously continued to have an impact in the northern areas of Canada, or the worker would never have asked for any disc numbers. It obviously could impact my application and above all the applications of my sons, my unknown grandmother's great grandsons. My sons deserved to know more than I did about their heritage when I was their age. My sons, like me, deserved to call themselves Inuk with confidence and understanding. My sons deserved something that I had never had.

I had to depend on my anaanatsiaq because my own mom lived a life without government documentation. She never had a driver's licence. She never had a passport. She never had a birth certificate. My mom arrived into a world where life was lived around the seasons of every year. There were no calendars or clocks when she was born above the treeline in the Keewatin district of northern Manitoba.

There were no maternity wards or doctors signing off on birth certificates. There was only each other and the every-day rhythm of survival. Life was about preparing for the next season. The next hunt. The next kill. Life was not about gathering up documents to prove that she was an Inuk. Life was about breathing in the moment.

The romanticism of that era was in reality all about making do for that day. Surviving the elements of snow and cold weather that was endless. I didn't have time to indulge in building a fantasy of what Angaviadniak's life would have looked like. I needed cold hard proof of her existence.

I began my own modern-day hunt. A hunt that meant using as many key words as I could think of and keying them into Google. A hunt that became a jumbled list of possible resources to review in libraries and on the web. A hunt that meant reaching out to strangers who could provide me with the pieces of me.

I had to start somewhere but the problem was that there was little existing information in print or living on the world wide web. The mystery of me had to be unravelled through a system that was no longer active. I had to start with a grand-mother of whom I had not one picture. I only had her name. The secret inside of my family hummed louder.

It made sense to begin with my grandfather, Cecil "Husky" Harris. My mom never spoke of him and always showed disdain on her face if his name was brought into a conversation with Auntie Frances. There were so many silences that lived inside of my mom. Silences that grew like hard stalagmites around parts of her heart.

All these northern people, people whose blood and genes had whirled and twirled their way into creating me, were people that I knew nothing about. Husky Harris was my grandfather and my only memory of him lay inside of me as a picture of a picture of him inside of a small frame. He was a tiny, wiry man with a dab of facial hair in the sepia photograph. He didn't look mean or rough. He looked healthy. I remember looking at him and trying to find a facial feature that resembled mine, but I couldn't see any. Years prior I had read about him. He was noted in the book because of a fifteen-year break from coming into any post to trade the furs he had trapped. I often thought about how he had assimilated backwards in the thinking of the Western world. He left behind the comforts of the white world to become fluent in Inuktitut, with three Inuk wives and three Inuk daughters.

I found him again in small writings that talked about a note he took from inside of a can left at a cairn[1] and how he had taken all three of his wives into Winnipeg to go shopping.[2] From what I could gather, he was seen as an oddity to those who were also employed through the Hudson's

---

1   MacDonald, "When the Caribou Failed," http://www.mhs.mb.ca /docs/mb_history/45/tolstoy.shtml.

2   Newman, *Merchant Princes*, 194.

Bay Company. I knew that he had died in 1940 and that he spoke with some of the foreign academics and explorers who arrived in the North seeking adventure. All the research I had done on him led me to one dead end after another. I could hear my mom's whispers of contempt arriving in my ears. I could hear her sighs of disdain. I gave up on my grandfather's very cold life trail.

I had to resort to books. Any book that mentioned the "disc" or "disk" system. I started to understand how the inconsistency in the spelling of a very small word could create duplications and confusion in research. I started to understand how misunderstood Inuit as a people were. I started to see neglect and how Inuit were positioned as a people who were more of an afterthought than as citizens of Canada who held value.

I had to give thought to those government administrators who birthed the disc system into the North. Why did they come up with a numbering system? How did anyone justify numbering Inuit? Why didn't they learn Inuktitut?

Most of all, I grew to understand why it was so difficult to find my anaanatsiaq, Angaviadniak.

CHAPTER THREE

akia

(The other side)

Between the years 2001 and 2008 I spent hours and hours online and in libraries. I was reading everything I could find about the Eskimo Identification Canada system even after my sons and I were granted membership into the Nunavut Land Claims Agreement in 2003. The question the woman had asked when I called North in the winter of 2001, "What was your mother's disc number?" haunted me. That one question stayed inside of me. Trying to find disc lists had become a secret obsession. There were so few lists that sat on public record or that were available through government archives.

In 2009 I became a full-time student with the Faculty of Native Studies at the University of Alberta. I was three months short of turning fifty-one when I entered post-secondary. It took me twenty-six months to complete my BA. In 2012 I was accepted into the inaugural master's degree program with the faculty. That acceptance allowed me the time and space to research the Eskimo Identification Canada system with access to more information than I had ever had previously. I fell in love with Cameron Library, the one library on campus that contained books devoted to the North. I have jokingly said to others, "I've read every book in here!" and while they are laughing, I stand in front of them thinking, "But I have!"

What I knew at the starting point of my research was that no one had ever sat down and written a book about the system. Many scholars had made mention of the system. Most of these scholars are non-Inuit and had encountered the system through their own interactions with Inuit. From what I could gather most of these same scholars and professionals saw the system as an innocent form of recordkeeping. A harmless form of managing the lives of a group of Natives who did not speak or think or react in the same way they did. Natives who needed the intervention of non-Inuit to bring organization to the disorganized. They may have seen themselves as "saviours to the downtrodden." For me, it was personal: the more I knew about the system, the closer I grew to my anaanatsiaq, and the better the chances became that I would find her.

One of the first points of my research was Pat Sandiford Grygier's 1997 book, *A Long Way from Home: The Tuberculosis Epidemic among the Inuit*. Grygier, a former federal employee with a degree in clinical psychology, makes mention of the disc system only in the foreword of an otherwise brilliant study on the treatment of Inuit during the first era of the illness. Grygier writes an explanation of the system as a simplistic way for white administrators and doctors to keep better records for their patients because Inuit names were difficult to spell, say, and manage. The white administrators noticed inconsistencies in the spelling of Inuit names and that reflected on their own inability to keep accurate medical records.

Grygier writes two lines clearly showing a non-Inuit view of the system: "Every Inuit was given a number, which was imprinted on a plastic disc that was usually worn around the neck or on the arm, like an army 'dog tag'...Thus, the first inhabitants of Canada were again ahead of the rest of us—in being issued with identification numbers" (49). What Grygier is reflecting on is that Inuit were numbered before the 1964 social insurance number program came into Canada and therefore this positioned Inuit at the top of the hierarchy of digital existence.

The system is presented as something that is unique and of benefit to the Inuit who are referred to as pioneers or influencers of the future. This is not the Inuit voice that is speaking but a non-Inuit health provider who is speaking from her vantage point. What is lacking is how the Inuit, those who lived the system, felt about it. What did they think of keeping a numbered identifier on their person at all times?

Wearing a numbered disc on your body is an inhuman and degrading form of treatment. This form of human management is in effect a breach of human rights, but more importantly, human dignity. The Universal Declaration of Human Rights clearly states in Article 5, "No one shall be subjected to torture or to cruel, inhuman or degrading treatment or punishment."[1] What I wonder is if the disc system became exempt from the provisions of the Declaration because it was introduced in 1941, before the Declaration was adopted? Can inhuman and degrading treatment of any human being be legally denied because Article 5 became active in 1948?

David Serkoak is an Inuit Elder, educator, and traditional drum-maker and dancer. He wrote in an email to me in 2013, "The government controlled us back then via RCMP, welfare agents and teachers we DO what we were told no questions asked...it was used for the Qablunaaq (white man) only...years later it began to bother me how the government treated us like their (bad) dogs." Serkoak is a man of few words, and his emotions are clearly on display. His animosity toward the government and other non-Inuit peoples of authority is evident. His capitalization of the word "DO" loudly demonstrates frustration toward a hidden system. As he grew older his interpretation of the disc system is compared to being a (bad) dog. An animal that is labelled or kept separate based on its behaviour or bad breeding, or his dog tag number.

Serkoak and Grygier offer opposing points of understanding of the disc system. Grygier sees the system in a positive light that launches Inuit Canadians into a futuristic mode of existence, while Serkoak's views show the distaste and the smouldering dislike of a respected Inuit Elder who

---

1   United Nations, *Universal Declaration of Human Rights*, Article 15.

had to live inside of the disc system. In other words, a different understanding between cause and effect. What needs to be explained is the cause.

KATIMAJUT — THEY ARE MEETING

The approach of the Inuit toward newcomers in the North was one of welcoming and song. Aaju Peter, Inuit lawyer, activist, sealskin designer and Inuit traditionalist, wrote:

> We wish for those coming to the area to have good experiences and have good thoughts about the place. By our actions we wish to show our gratitude for the area, for the land, the game, etc. thereby ensuring that the land will continue to provide for our needs and that when we go to the area of those who visited, we will be treated in like manner. The feeling is positive, that of gratitude, respect and sharing. An Elder welcomes the visitors by singing ancient songs that tell about awareness, hunting, the environment and respect.[2]

Inuit welcomed visitors with warmth and open heartedness. They saw the coming to shore of those who did not look like them as an opportunity to welcome them through song.

---

2   Peter, "Inuit Use and Occupation," 43.

Visitors were to be celebrated. Inuit treated the visitors as people of importance and honour. Visitors were welcomed to Inuit lands and homes with good feelings. The purpose being that Inuit wanted to give the visitors good memories to carry back to their homes.

This welcoming of visitors is called tunnganarniq. It is one of the traditional and inherent values of Inuit Qaujimajatuqangit or IQ that is important for buildings positive relationships.[3]

Inuit did not view visitors as people of mistrust or suspicion. The extension of kindness is essential to the Inuit soul. Visitors were not seen as dangerous or harmful but as people who were in need of food, rest and all the comfort that an Inuit community could provide. Adhering to IQ values is the essence of Inuit life. Being kind is part of what lies inside of every Inuk.

From the Inuit worldview what the non-Inuit needed was to eat, rest and reassemble themselves after a long journey. Non-Inuit were not to be put into a place of nervousness or unease. Early history is written by non-Inuit whose renderings are from their perspective. Non-Inuit saw the North as a place to explore. Secondly it was a place to harvest and lay claim to even though they had been welcomed warmly and treated fairly.

---

3   "Inuit Societal Values," Representative for Children and Youth, Government of Nunavut, https://rcynu.ca/what-guides-us/inuit -societal-values.

Overall, Indigenous Canadians never saw land as a possession. Land was for everyone, and land was to be shared. Indigenous expectations were as stewards and not owners of the land. Nor was land something that needed to be tamed or controlled. Land was a friend, not an enemy.

Initially non-Inuit did not share that same sort of value toward land. There is one word that is a constant in the Canadian North, and it remains active in present day. It is the word "sovereignty." Both the Inuit and the non-Inuit continue to seek out a definition for this word. The *Canadian Encyclopedia* offers a good working definition of sovereignty: "Sovereignty is an abstract legal concept. It also has political, social and economic implications. In strictly legal terms, sovereignty describes the power of a state to govern itself and its subjects. In this sense, sovereignty is the highest source of the law."[4] When it comes to Indigenous People in Canada and Inuit, sovereignty becomes complex. Governor General Mary Simon uses the idiom of self-government to describe a history of unwritten laws, deeply inscribed, and the difficulty of "convincing today's governments that we were once a self-governing people."[5]

Prior to non-Inuit arriving in the North, the Inuktitut language did not contain the word "sovereignty" because

4   Edward Watson McWhinney, "Sovereignty," *The Canadian Encyclopedia*, https://www.thecanadianencyclopedia.ca/en/article/sovereignty#.

5   Mary Simon, *Inuit: One Future—One Arctic*, 74.

Inuit never would have seen anyone as holding supreme power over a community of people or land. Since the establishment of the Nunavut government, a word has been birthed into Inuktitut existence. It is "aulatsigunnarniq." It quite literally means "'the ability to make things move' in the context of being able to control something."[6]

What I needed was the ability to make things move at the enrolment office in Nunavut, to find my grandmother's disc number. It seemed so simple back in 2001. I did not realize then that it would take a lifetime of research to understand sovereignty and to understand how the state arrived at a numbered tagging system for the Inuit and how that gave the Canadian government representatives the "ability to make things move."

---

6   Baldassarri, Elene. "The Northwest Passage as a Question of Sovereignty." The Environment & Society Portal. 2012. https://www.environmentandsociety.org/exhibitions/northwest-passage/northwest-passage-question-sovereignty.

a'nirmaqtuq

(*It hurts*)

Inuit Canadians were accustomed to Qallunaat, meaning non-Inuit who John Amagoalik describes as "people who jump to conclusions and don't have any patience and always want to do things right now," coming and going in and out of their lives.[1] Contact between Inuit and Qallunaat was established through a series of seasonal short-term stays by non-Inuit based on exploration and whaling.

The grand narrative of Canada venerates the early explorers of our country. There was one instance in the year 1577 in Arctic history that is an example of how Inuit became living proof of Martin Frobisher's explorations. Inuit were used as concrete proof of his travels when Frobisher kidnapped an Inuit man and an Inuit woman, unknown to one another, and her child. He took them home to Queen Elizabeth I. This resulted in the Russian ambassador to London filing a formal complaint because he thought the Inuit Canadians were Tartars from Mongolia.[2] It is evidence of how Frobisher's Inuit captives became commodities that caused a political

---

1   Sandiford, *Qallunaat!: Why White People are Funny*, 2006.

2   Dorais, *The Language of the Inuit*, 88.

rift. Frobisher used three Inuit people as samples or specimens to be placed before Queen Elizabeth I, the funder of his work. While he harvested minerals, he also harvested humans in the North of Canada. Inuit were living souvenirs of his travels. All three died shortly after their arrival to England. According to Zebedee Nungak, these inhuman interactions are an example of how "Inuit sovereignty in the Arctic started being systematically undermined long before there was regular, sustained contact with civilization."[3]

To an early explorer not only was the land and its resources up for grabs but the Inuit were as well. Being treated as less than human is a constant theme projected toward Inuit Canadians and seeing the early roots of that attitude provides a preview to future non-Inuit administrators and the attitude they brought northward.

As the account of one of the Queen's subjects, Martin Frobisher, kidnapping three Inuit and the threat of a Russian interloper laying claim to those same bodies illustrates, "sovereignty" and what it meant where the Canadian Arctic and its inhabitants were concerned has been something Inuit have wrestled with since the sixteenth century. These intrusions into Inuit sovereignty form the roots of Canadian military involvement in the North, a fact that is later exposed in Canadian military history through the First and Second World Wars and the Cold War with the development of the Distant Early Warning (DEW) Line.

---

3   Nungak, "The Decimation of Inuit Security."

It was not until non-Inuit took up residency in the Arctic that Inuit traditional life was examined and questioned. Once non-Inuit became permanent citizens in the Arctic, Inuit traditional life was forced into unwanted change.

After Frobisher's first forays into Inuit lands, the first outsiders to arrive and lay colonial influence onto Inuit culture were the Moravians who set up the Nain Mission Station in Labrador in 1771. More than a century later, the Catholic and Anglican missionaries appeared. Christianity started laying down its deep northern roots. While the mission people were setting up permanent homes, their intrusion was accompanied by "the spread of trading posts and the establishment of RCMP posts across the Arctic" that "brought once and for all the white man with his institutions, his bureaucracy and his passion for order."[4]

In my search for my grandmother's disc number, I realized yet again how important it is to understand this history of incursion into Inuit sovereignty. I needed a thorough understanding of this history to know where to look. In *Eskimo Identification and Disc Numbers: A Brief History*, Barry Roberts provides an accurate description that foreshadows the implementation of the disc system. He clearly states that the white administrators saw only an empty landscape that required taming. Non-Inuit administrators peppered the landscape with wooden structures while putting people inside churches and tasking office

---

4   Roberts, *Eskimo Identification*, 1.

administrators with bringing "order" to what they saw as the jumbled tundra. Inside of this order lay the disc system that on the outside appeared like a quick and easy solution for the administrators who would be held accountable to the federal government. Easy is never best.

- The Canadian Arctic prior to the 1900s was a place of global exploration and harvesting of minerals and wildlife. Diamond Jenness described the North as an example of "government myopia" or short-sightedness. The Canadian government was moving about and making a profit on lands deemed a part of Canada and in the process creating and recreating colonial methods of conquering an Inuit population that it thought needed to be brought into modern-day living and thinking.

After 1900 and the loss of land in the Alaska boundary dispute, the Canadian government felt it needed to affirm its claim to the North more concretely. In 1903, it dispatched a ship named the *Neptune* to the Arctic: "[C]oncurrent with the extension of police authority to Herschel Island in the western Arctic and Fort McPherson in the Mackenzie River valley, the *Neptune* Expedition headed north to enforce Canadian jurisdiction in the...Arctic."[5] The goal of this voyage was to assert non-Inuit domination in the Hudson Bay through the use of the North-West Mounted Police (later the RCMP) who would put into practice non-Inuit customs, laws, taxation, and prevent the killing of endangered species,

---

5   Ross, "Canadian Sovereignty in the Arctic," 90.

mainly the muskox. However, most importantly this voyage was made to introduce the Inuit to King Edward VII as the ruler over their existence, as Ross points out in his account of an interaction between the NWMP and the Inuit during the *Neptune* Expedition:

> In a comical fashion Superintendent J.D. Moodie, a member of the RCMP, gathers a group of twenty-five Inuit in the western Arctic, in an area some 500 miles away from Churchill, by sea, to tell them "...there was a big chief over them all who had many tribes of different colours and how this big chief, King Edward wanted them all to do what was right and good..." This meeting is appropriately called by Doctor Borden, the medical officer on board the Neptune, "the pow-wow at Govt. House."[6]

In this account, Moodie displays what continues to be common in the minds of government officials that all Indigenous peoples are the same and that Inuit people carried out the same forms of leadership as the prairie First Nations of Canada. It is a blatant misconception that would return to irk the government in later years. In celebration of this meeting the superintendent gave each Inuit adult male the gift of a pair of woollen underwear.[7] The

---

6   Ross, "Canadian Sovereignty in the Arctic," 100.

7   Ross, "Canadian Sovereignty in the Arctic," 100.

reaction of the Inuit to this meeting according to Borden was "standing open-mouthed with varied expressions" during Moodie's speech:

> Their amazement is not difficult to understand. They had experienced encounters with white explorers for a century and a half. For more than forty years they had maintained close economic and social ties with American and Scottish whalemen. Their hunting equipment included whaleboats, harpoon guns, shoulder guns firing explosive projectiles, and repeating rifles. They wore American shirts, trousers, jackets, overalls, hats and sunglasses. Their women used sewing machines and possessed ball gowns for dances. And here was underwear proffered like frankincense and myrrh, accompanied by a fairy tale about a Big Chief. They were speechless.[8]

Borden's sarcasm highlights the understandings of Moodie, a white law enforcer and someone who gained more and more power over the daily lives of Inuit Canadians during his time as superintendent. We can see the influence of western styles of clothing that have infiltrated Inuit life along with tools that were no longer handmade. Moodie's point of view is that all Indigenous peoples operated in tribes with chiefs—a system that Inuit never had. Inuit operated

8   Ross, "Canadian Sovereignty in the Arctic," 100–101.

within very small groupings and "Inuit became leaders by gaining a respect from the people of their camps, not by getting elected. A respected man was someone who the people looked up to for direction and for the right decisions when they had to be made."[9] The concept of having someone in the position of leadership was accepted in times of need only but that person was not called "chief." That word may have been as much of a mystery to the Inuit as was the gifting of woollen underwear.

Most importantly, what must be recognized from this interaction between Moodie and the Inuit is the amount of ignorance that Moodie carried toward Inuit culture and understandings as well as the early beginnings of non-Inuit power and dominance.

TASITAQPUQ — BEGINS TO STRETCH, EXTEND

Aside from the treatment toward the Inuit as though they were northern First Nations, it must be recognized that Inuit people in Canada, other than the Inuit of Labrador, were never invited or negotiated into treaty-making in any form. It must also be made clear that the NWMP, through the voyage of the *Neptune*, were now placed into the North as the authority figures representing the "Big Chief" and the Canadian state. In 1903 the government of Canada had accomplished

---

9   Arnaquq, "Uqaujjuusiat," 13.

what it had wanted to do since the earliest incursions into Inuit sovereignty: it had placed a British figurehead into the conscience of the Inuit and had provided men in uniform as a constant reminder of the state's sovereign power and authority. Inuit were placed into a position of submission.

World War I raged across the ocean from 1914–1918 and while the Canadian government was involved in sending over thousands of Canadian troops, they were at the same time enforcing the war measures power of the Crown through the War Measures Act. The Act affected all Indigenous Canadians. It gave the Crown full power over all its citizenry and allowed the government to ban social gatherings. For the First Nations of the western Canadian provinces, all dances and ceremonies were disallowed; this same ban reached the Canadian Arctic by the late 1920s.[10] However, a point of distinction between how the law was applied to First Nations and to Inuit is best made by Alethea Arnaquq-Baril, Inuit filmmaker and producer of Unikkaat Studios Inc., located in Iqaluit, NU, who stated that the Inuit transition into modern-day life through colonization was akin to moving from "the ice age to the space age" meaning that colonization occurred later and faster for Inuit in comparison to First Nations or Métis of Canada.[11]

---

10   Wilson, "Indian Act Timeline," 85–86.

11   Arnaquq-Baril, Alethea. "Tunniitt: Retracing the Lines of Inuit Tattoos." Unikkaat Studios Inc, 2012. http://www.unikkaat.com /projects/tunniit-retracing-the-lines-of-inuit-tattoos/.

What Arnaquq-Baril points out is that assimilative policies and forces were at work across Canada but in the Arctic
colonial interference through law ran at an accelerated
pace. There was a rapidity in outlawing Inuit traditional
practices such as the Inuktitut language, drum dancing
ceremonies and facial tattooing by women. While Status
First Nations continue to be governed by the Indian Act,
Inuit were treated with the same heavy handedness, but
without an Act to regulate the treatment. Inuit traditional
practices became illegal and within a generation, the close
link between practices like tattooing and drumming and
traditional naming practices was lost. My hope is that the
story of how I reclaimed my Inuit identity will help restore
these links and give others a link to their identity.

Inuit are not members of the Indian Act, but the Indian
Act maintains a strong influence over how Inuit continue to
be treated by the Canadian state. There remains no formal
parliamentary piece of legislation pertaining exclusively to
Inuit nor has the Canadian government ever defined the
word "Inuit." Instead, in the northern areas of Canada power
presented itself in different physical forms. This is more evident in the widespread building of RCMP posts that began to
clutter the shoreline of the Hudson's Bay. Colonialism was
seeping its way into the daily lives of Inuit.

Arnaquq-Baril released her movie *Tunniit: Retracing
the Lines* as a documentary that examines the extinction
of facial tattooing by Inuit women. The act of facial tattooing was exclusive to Inuit women; men never tattooed their

faces, hands, wrists, forearms or thighs. There is ceremony and teaching of taboos attached to the tattooing process as described by Gaul:

> Some say the tattooist probably prayed with every stitch, sometimes rubbing the soot in with her finger or a poker. She would gently remind the girl that the sea goddess denied access to the afterlife to women whose fingers weren't tattooed. Women without face tattoos were banished to *noqurmiut*, "the land of the crestfallen" where they spent an eternity with their heads hanging down, smoke bellowing out of their throats.[12]

The sea goddess in the above quote is Sedna, one of the most storied and often the meanest of goddesses within Inuit legend. Imagine an elderly Inuit woman whispering to a young girl her possible fate if she did not tattoo. Without the lines on her fingers, she would never settle in one of the afterlands that Inuit believe in. Without facial tattoos she would spend her next life with her head hanging forward, blowing smoke from her lungs. Her shame and humiliation would be on display to everyone who had gone before her and to those who arrive after her. A lack of tattoos meant being shunned forever. The tattooist provided the story of the ceremony of tattooing to the next generation. Death for

---

12   Gaul, "Between the Lines," XXX.

Inuit was never the end of life but the beginning to a new life and to be shunned from that new life is the highest form of Inuit punishment.

There is an intimate cultural beauty within the process. The comfort of an older woman passing on her wisdom to a young girl who would in the future do the same in a kudlik-lit tent or igloo. The traditional tattooist would be hand-stitching the stories of the young girl's ancestors onto her body to distract her from the pain of tattooing while embedding Inuit oral history into her memory.

Kaj Birket-Smith, in *Caribou Eskimos, Material and Social Life and their Cultural Position* in 1929, reinforced the disappearance of the tattooing practice amongst the Padlimiut Inuit. Tattooing was something he found only when he travelled farther away from populated posts. Birket-Smith felt that the Padlimiut Inuit women were the least civilized of all the Inuit he had encountered and observed. He noted that unlike coastal Inuit women at Eskimo Point and Sentry Island who were not tattooed, the inland Padlimiut women were.[13]

I am Padlimiut. Padlei Inuit were often portrayed as the least colonized and civilized of all Inuit in Canada. According to Birket-Smith, the Padlei women who had sustained contact with non-Inuit were no longer tattooing but those who were farther away continued the practice as a rite of womanhood. The removal of visible lines from an Inuk woman's

---

13   Birket–Smith, *The Caribou Eskimos*, 228–29.

face and hands is another example of the power non-Inuit have exerted over Inuit. That a traditional practice becomes illegal or a transgression according to Christianity is an indication of how Inuit were fearful of the white men and women who were invading their daily lives.

It has taken Inuit women over one hundred years to place tunniit back into everyday practice. Jana Angulalik in a 2021 article describes the meaning of tattoos:

> Tattoos on the thighs are birthing tattoos. They prepare a baby to enter the world in beauty and knowledge, born between traditionally marked thighs. Our tattoos mark milestones and triumphs, but they can also represent loved ones who are no longer with us, or stories that are difficult to share.[14]

There may be lines tattooed onto present-day Inuit women that represent the stories that are too difficult to speak, the stories that tell of Inuit shaming and sin because a grandmother dared to practice her cultural beliefs. The heavy hand of those in authority becomes heavier.

Just as birthing tattoos keep the link between generations close to the body, so drum dances are a link between the present generations and the ancestors. Banning these activities has done as much harm to Inuit by obscuring traditional naming practices as the disc system did. Drum

---

14   Angulalik, "Behind the Inuit Tattoo Revival."

dances in the Canadian Arctic were a time of social gathering and a time of spiritual reconnection, a time of giving thanks back to the land and what it had provided and would continue to provide. K. Patricia Dewar received her doctorate from the University of Alberta in 1990. She completed her PhD research on Inuit drum dancing and found that

> The spiritual function of the dance did not elude the early explorers and anthropologists...They recognized its spirituality, but vigorously opposed its practice since it did not conform to the teaching and rituals of the Church. Remarks made by Euro-Americans reveal a belief that they held a monopoly not only on "real" religion but also on "real" dance.[15]

Inuit do not drum in the manner of First Nations. An Inuit drum or qilaut is never struck in the centre. The tones and echoes are formed from the striking of the outside rim with a qatuk, a wooden stick. Inuit would drum dance to call on the spirits for guidance with an upcoming hunt or time of fishing or for protection when times were tough. It was a time of gathering together to connect respectfully with the spirit world through song and drum. Drumming represented a time of prayer and singing to the spirits who would help with the harvesting of meat and fish to be stored for winter meals.

---

15   Dewar, "You Had To Be There," 20–29.

David Serkoak, a 69-year-old, present-day drum dance instructor, Elder and cultural leader from the Keewatin area of northern Manitoba, has his story recounted in Margo Pfieff's *Nilliajut: Inuit Perspectives on Security*: "One night when he was six or seven...a drum dance was happening in the family's tent. Suddenly, the police broke in, restrained his father, broke his drum and tossed it aside. The ancient tradition of drum dancing had become a sin."[16] Serkoak is a Barrenlands Inuk of Ahiamiut or Padlei descent. He is like me, a Caribou Inuk. He is one of my own. What his memory shows is that around 1959 in Canada the presence of the RCMP in the North and the law that they were enforcing was again trying to remove Inuit traditional spiritual practices. While traditions were being banned in the North as late as 1959, the Northwest Coastal First Nations groups who were banned from potlatch ceremonies in 1884 had that ban lifted by 1951.[17] Assimilation in the North is truly happening much later and faster in comparison to First Nations in Canada who are reclaiming traditional practices and able to teach future generations.

The intergenerational effect of asserting state sovereignty over the North can be illustrated succinctly by observing language loss among Inuit. The effects of breaking

---

16   Pfieff, "A Man of Principle," 23.

17   René Gadacz, "Potlatch." *The Canadian Encyclopedia*, February 7, 2006, last edited October 24, 2019. https://www .thecanadianencyclopedia.ca/en/article/potlatch.

Inuit traditional transference of language and cultural practices remain obvious. The Inuktitut language is currently
in use at a rate of approximately 65 per cent in Nunavut
and is the first language of many Nunavummiut households.
Inuktitut was in use 100 per cent of the time less than a generation ago. This means that the interruption of Inuktitut
language transmission through the generations is visible:
Within two generations, Inuit lost 35 per cent of the use of
their mother tongue. A widespread failure of language transference when those in power stop being those who first lived
on the land.

Reviewing the usage of the Inuktitut language, the
disappearance and revitalization of Inuit women's facial tattooing and the outlawing of drum dancing frames the power
that the white man carried into Canada's North. When language, ceremony and spiritual connections are being sliced,
outlawed, and categorized as sin, the invasiveness of the
colonizer cutting into Inuit daily lives is like watching a slow
and painful death.

The removal of Inuit essence is attacked further
through the ease with which the Eskimo Identification
Canada system slid into existence. The system was a simple next step for the non-Inuit administrators of Inuit lives.
The system was ushered into the North without national
headlines or an announcement in the House of Commons
and as such it remains absent from the canons of Canadian
history. It is a system that was exclusive to Inuit Canadians.
While there have been other numbering systems applied

to Indigenous People around the world, these were generally used for specific purposes or for limited duration; the Eskimo Identification System Canada controlled every aspect of Inuit lives for three decades. This sets it apart from any other system. It is a system that the Inuit have never received a formal apology for. The federal government has yet to acknowledge the harm it caused.

. I do not write this book with anger, which is an emotion that Inuit rarely express. Instead, this writing explores the need for tukitaaqtuq, an Inuktitut word meaning, "They explain to one another, reach understanding, receive an explanation from the past." I have purposely chosen this Inuktitut word because I have found only two Canadian government-sponsored documents written by government-paid writers about the Eskimo Identification Canada system and one government document concerning Inuit policy in Canada that does not make mention of this system at all. The voice of the Inuit disc holders, the words of those most affected, the Inuit themselves, is not expressed, published, or documented.

Community leader and the first Inuk politician to sit in the Northwest Territories Legislative Assembly, Abraham Okpik, once said, "A hungry stomach has no rules!"[18] and the bellies of Inuit peoples and their life experiences growl boldly for inclusion in the annals of not only the grand narrative of Canadian history but the grand narrative of Indigenous Canadian history.

---

18 Okpik, *We Call it Survival*, 51.

In my story so far, we have seen how the Canadian government marched in and took over. By the early 1920s, Inuit had sovereignty only over the one thing that was theirs to keep—their name. But even that was under threat. To complete the story of the disc system, we first have to understand how the attitude of militancy was developed in Canada and can only do so by panning back and reviewing the history of both a national and international timeline.

As reflected in previous Inuit history, the state first began laying the groundwork and later entrenchment of its sovereignty in the late 1920s by having the Inuit use biblical names for the sake of the religious sacrament of baptism and for the sake of the non-Inuit administrators who were in the North trying to sort out who the Inuit were. Inuit did take the biblical names but chose to "Inuiticize" them by turning names like "Adam" into "Atami," "Luke" into "Lucasi" and "Jessie" into "Siasi." These names were first prescribed by the mission people while each Inuit still used "a second (Eskimo) one anyway. But to others just beginning to arrive in the Arctic—the traders, policemen and, doctors etc. who were stumped by the absence of surnames and either unable or unwilling to learn the distinguishing name—the new method only compounded an already difficult problem."[19]

In 1924 Minister of the Interior Charles Stewart requested that an amendment to the Indian Act of 1876 be accepted by Canadian parliament, stating "the

---

19   Roberts, *Eskimo Identification*, 2.

Superintendent General of Indian Affairs shall have charge of Eskimo Affairs."[20] This was the first time that the Inuit of Canada had ever been recognized in Canadian legislation. The bill passed. However, unlike the First Nations of Canada, the Inuit were not recognized as wards of the state but as Canadian citizens and by 1928 authority over the Inuit was given to the Department of Indian Affairs of the Northwest Territories (NWT) Council. As Canadian citizens, the Inuit were given the right to vote, though "from 1905 to 1951 there were no representative political institutions in the Northwest Territories...Technically, Inuit could vote in territorial elections, but as there were no seats in their areas, the right was purely formal" and as far as participating in federal elections, "polling stations were not established for all communities before the 1962 federal election."[21] By this law, Inuit were not wards of the state and were given the power to participate in territorial and federal elections, yet this was done without giving Inuit a representative to vote for or a place to go and cast a ballot. State sovereignty, at times, is superficial.

In 1930, the Canadian government repealed this amendment, but Inuit administration continued under the NWT Council in Ottawa and by the Royal Canadian Mounted Police.[22] From 1930 onward the Canadian state had the responsibility of providing relief to the Inuit and it was at

---

20   Tester and Kulchyski, *Tammarniit*, 19.

21   Campbell, *Sovereignty and Citizenship*, 38.

22   Bonesteel, "The E-Number Identification System," 6.

this point, from 1933 to 1939, that the names of the Inuit again fell under the scrutiny of the NWT bureaucrats and members of the RCMP.

The main players are revealed in a series of communications between government representatives and enforcers of the law. H.H. Rowatt, deputy minister, Department of the Interior of the NWT, first received a letter on June 26, 1933, from the chairman of the Dominion Lands Board requesting a standardization of spelling of all Inuit names. This idea was reinforced by a report written by Dr. J.A. Bildfell, who was working on the health conditions of the Inuit as part of the 1933 Eastern Arctic Expedition. Bildfell's contribution to the disc system was to introduce fingerprinting Inuit as a form of identification as the standardization of spelling seems impossible.

However, by 1935 only seventeen Inuit had been fingerprinted. Major D.L. McKeand, Department of the Interior, who became the major player in the implementation of the disc system, stepped in on April 11, 1935, with a letter to J. Lorne Turner, director of lands, NWT and Yukon Branch. In his letter, McKeand reinforced the concept of Inuit names being difficult for administrators and mentioned the possibility of issuing numeric tags to all Inuit as was previously suggested by Dr. A.G. McKinnon, a medical officer on Baffin Island.

Dr. McKinnon and Turner exchanged two more letters concerning the look of the disc and how the numeric system would appear on each disc and whether or not the image of a crown or bison should be placed in the centre of each disc. It is interesting that the administrators could even toy with the image of a bison, an animal that is not found anywhere in the Arctic and therefore not an animal associated with Inuit but instead with First Nations. The more I dug into colonial records to find my grandmother's disc number, the more I saw such ignorance of the non-Inuit on display.

Major McKeand made a formal request for discs on September 8, 1936, to Roy A. Gibson, assistant deputy minister, Department of Lands and Resources. A four-year break then ensued, but the bureaucrats had already prepared and formulated the disc system and while their paperwork was being filed and made complete, and the surveyors of the land were hard at work creating health and registration districts.

Armed with this information, I decided to start looking for my anaanatsiaq in the land of her ancestors. The one thing the colonial government and European explorers had done repeatedly was to map out the North to assist them in marking "their" territory. Now, I thought, these maps could finally be of some use other than exploitation. Prior to the forced relocations of all Inuit in the 1950s, a time when Inuit were dubbed "human flagpoles"[23]—as they represented

---

23   Campion-Smith, Bruce. "Ottawa Apologizes to Inuit for Using them as 'Human Flagpoles,'" *The Star*, August 18, 2010. https://www.thestar.com/news/canada/2010/08/18/ottawa _apologizes_to_inuit_for_using_them_as_human _flagpoles.html.

the flagstaffs or living proof of Canada's sovereignty in the North—my original home territory was the Keewatin area of northern Manitoba.

I obtained maps dated 1926 through to 1939. I was looking for the building-up of RCMP and trading posts, with the emphasis on the Keewatin district. From there, I hoped, I could trace my grandmother's whereabouts, as she would have had to report to one of these posts to get her disc. The early years in my range covered the approximate time of my mother's birth, and I was hopeful that by concentrating on that time, I would be able to find some reference to either her or my anaanatsiaq's whereabouts. The first map (Appendix 1) dated 1926 was prepared by the Department of the Interior and shows that there was at the time only one RCMP post in the Keewatin area, located at Chesterfield Inlet, along with one post office. The map shows six HBC trading posts and three HBC outposts scattered throughout the district. In 1929 (Appendix 2) again there is only one RCMP post at Chesterfield, but by now there were thirteen trading posts. This signals the expansion of the fur trade and a heavier presence of non-Indigenous people in the area. Non-Inuit power in the North was becoming more visible, and every new post that was marked on a map made my search more complicated.

By 1939, according to the map produced by the Department of Mines and Resources (Appendix 3), three RCMP posts had been established in the Keewatin area, one in Baker Lake, one in Eskimo Point, and one in Chesterfield

Inlet. According to Kirt Ejesiak, the Canadian government's official reason for multiplying RCMP posts was "to save the Inuit from harm but the fact was that they had concerns related to sovereignty, which was never revealed to the Inuit."[24] I equate this exercise to having strangers enter my home and taking it over. They aren't telling me why they have taken over. As time passes, my home is no longer my own and my freedoms are limited to doing what pleases the invaders. My only function is to keep breathing so that those who have taken over appear to serve an important and necessary purpose.

Because of the physical placement of RCMP posts, RCMP constables were put in charge of the distribution of the discs. They also served as the administrators of the system as they maintained disc lists and reported that information back to Ottawa. They were the enforcers of the disc system.

In 1939 (Appendix 4) a map prepared by the Department of Mines and Resources designated Eskimo Registration Districts. In heavy, black bold lines these maps mark E1–E9 for the Eastern Arctic Eskimos and W1–W14 for Western Arctic Eskimos. The map covers the Northwest Territories, extending to just below the Arctic Islands and covers the northern half of Quebec. The map changes in 1941 (Appendix 5), and at the time the disc system is introduced, districts W4–14 no longer existed. Is this because the Canadian government came to the realization that the bulk of the Inuit

---

24   Ejesiak, "An Arctic Inuit Union," 70–75.

population was north of Norman Wells and around Aklavik, and that they had created a cartographic faux pas? I do not know, but I do know that every time I looked at the maps, the ignorance of the mapmakers and administrators seemed to become more evident.

SAATTUQ – BEGINS TO FACE OR PUT SOMETHING IN FRONT OF SOMEONE, ACCUSES

By 1941, the administrators were ready to launch the disc system, boundaries and borders had been drawn, discs had been manufactured, and all was in readiness. At last there would no longer be a need to deal with Inuit names. As a reinforcement, in 1939 the Supreme Court of Canada declared Inuit are indeed the responsibility of the federal government in the court case Reference Re Eskimos.[25] This is a case filed by the province of Quebec forcing the issue of who was to pick up the tab on the medical care of the Inuit— the federal government or the province?

In the view of the province of Quebec, Inuit fell under federal jurisdiction and should be budgeted as such. This question first hit the courts in 1935 and in 1937 and after two years of preparation, there were displays of First Nations and Inuit skulls, photographs and clothing filling a Supreme Court courtroom along with ethnographers,

---

25   Reference Re Eskimos.

lawyers and justices Duff, Cannon, Kerwin, Davis, Hudson, and Crocket.[26]

As the court debated the definition of an Indian as opposed to the definition of an Eskimo, with neither First Nations nor Inuit peoples present in the courtroom, Auguste Desilets, a lawyer for the federal government, famously stated:

> He was prepared to concede that "Eskimos" dif-
> fered from "aborigines" in their clothing, food, fuel,
> winter dwellings, and hunting practices. However,
> if one scrutinized the "main characters of their life"
> Desilets insisted, it was clear that "Eskimos" were
> exactly like Indians. Both groups exhibited, stated
> Desilets, "the same dependence upon fish and
> game for subsistence, the same lack of any organ-
> ization for agriculture and industrial production, the
> same absence for exchange of wealth by way of
> money, the same poverty, the same ignorance, the
> same unhygienic mode of existence."[27]

It is not until April of 1939 that the Supreme Court of Canada concluded that Inuit were the responsibility of the federal government; that same year, on September 1, World War II broke out. As the war drew on and Germany invaded

---

26   Reference Re Eskimos.

27   Qtd in Backhouse, *Colour Coded,* 41.

the Soviet Union in 1941, the matter of state sovereignty over the Canadian Arctic became a matter of international importance and for the Canadian government, exerting their sovereignty meant establishing more formal control over the population of the North.

In 1941, along with the decennial census, the disc containing the words "Eskimo Identification Canada" and looped onto a leather-like piece of string became a point for discussion with the NWT Council. This point is listed under item (7) (x) 7717 on the agenda (Appendix 6). It falls into the area of "Arctic Matters" and is listed after "Scout Eric Liddell" and before "Tourist traffic in the Arctic" and is given a total of six sentences in the minutes of the meeting. The matter is discussed by six non-Inuit men.[28] There were no Inuit at the meeting.

The chairman opened with remarks about the continued confusion surrounding the identification of "Eskimos and maintaining records of their hunting, education, hospitalization and relief because of the differences in spelling names."[29] Dr. McGill made a point of referencing that "Indians were given a number and a check was kept of them at Treaty time but he realized this could not be done with Eskimos because there was no tribal system or Treaty payments."[30]

---

28   Roberts, *Eskimo Identification*, 12–15.

29   NWT Council 1941).

30   (NWT Council, Appendix 7).

The secretary then reported that field officers and missionaries were in agreement with the disc system and that naval identification discs had been secured and were tabled for inspection by members of council. The secretary indicated that discs, to be worn around the neck, retailed between $2.75 and $3.00 per thousand. Commissioner Wood remarked that 1941 "would be the most appropriate time to introduce the system because an issue could be made when the census was being taken."[31] A short discussion on the appearance of the discs ensued, with a suggestion that either the Canadian Coat of Arms or His Majesty's likeness would be preferred, and all agreed that the Department of State should be consulted.

The minutes record that Dr. McGill moved the motion, Commissioner Wood seconded "that the system of identification discs for Eskimos be approved."[32] The motion was carried. The legislative notes and evidence point to the fact that the process of determining sovereignty over Inuit took less than five minutes. Short, and simple. A brief amount of time that has affected Inuit Canadians for generations.

On March 14, 1941, a little more than a month later, "Arctic Matters" sits as item 13 on the NWT Council agenda with Article (v) showing as "Eskimo identification discs" (Appendix 8). In this session the disc system is given a total of three sentences. As reported in the minutes of the meeting, "likeness of the King or the Great Seal of Canada could

---

31 (NWT Council).

32 (NWT Council).

not be used. However, the secretary of state saw no objection to the use of the Canadian Coat of Arms to be distributed to all Eskimos in Canada."

PIGIALIRQIPAA – BEGINS AGAIN

Canada's North might not have taken on the strategic power that it did if it had not been for World War II. The North became a place of possibilities that required protection and in the defence of this northern border the Canadian state was placed in the position of knowing the landscape fully. While the Inuit remained numbered spectres of the tundra, the state worked hard at guarding and securing a border that previously was a place of neutrality and impartiality.

In 1941 Prentice G. Downes, an American professor, was hired by the military as a cartographer. He was sent into the Keewatin region, more specifically to Nueltin Lake, to map the lake and surrounding area. He released his book *Sleeping Island: The Story of One Man's Travels in the Great Barren Lands of the Canadian North* in 1942. The book contained maps of Nueltin and surrounding area. In 1944 Downes was criticized by Trevor Lloyd in a book review for what appeared to be unfinished sketches and a lack of accuracy. Downes replied that he was employed as a cartographer during a time when a German invasion through the Hudson Straits and Bay was a fearsome possibility. Based on that fear he intentionally produced inaccurate maps with the thinking that if someone needed accurate information, they would seek secondary sources as well.[33]

Downes's maps demonstrate the strategic power of the North during the War, as well as the paranoia that was racing through the country at that time. When a professional is instructed to intentionally produce and publish inaccurate work, the sovereignty of the state becomes an item of controlled protection and a display of public inexactness. Not once did anyone consider how these inaccurate maps might harm Inuit and affect their safety. These inaccurate maps struck close to home—such deliberate misinformation didn't just remain within the sphere of the war. After the war, Padlei Inuit were forcibly relocated to Nueltin Lake and for someone like me who was searching for my ancestors, misinformation added another layer of complexity to my journey. But to the state, creating inaccurate maps mattered more than the safety of the people who lived there.

During the course of the war years the disc system experienced problems of its own in its own inexactness. Midway through 1941 Major McKeand noted that a report about the disc issuance by the "R.C.M. Police" of the Pangnirtung Detachment indicated that "not one identification number is given. I would not suggest that these be returned to the R.C.M. Police for completion but I would like to have an opportunity of discussing the matter with Inspector Martin to ascertain if it would be possible to add the identification

---

33   Downes, *Sleeping Island*, 301.

numbers without too much inconvenience."[34] McKeand notes that the disc number was to be used for "keeping track of (a) hunting (b) trapping (c) education (d) hospitalization and (e) misdemeanours, etc."[35] It is interesting to note how the uses of the disc system had expanded since the original list of uses for the disc system noted in the February 11, 1941, NWT Council session, and now included as a final item in McKeand's list using the disc to track compliance with the law. Imposing colonial sovereignty over Inuit requires lists and more tasks to make lists for. Sovereignty in this context becomes micro-management.

Other problems began to pop up as the system struggled to entrench itself into Inuit life. Sergeant H.S. Covell of Aklavik reported that he had no discs because the RCMP of the area took on the role of census takers though this was supposed to be done by Dr. D. Livingstone. Livingstone was allotted 300 discs for the area and the census was completed without all Inuit receiving their discs. While the system was being implemented and administrative problems were being discussed by officials, those who were doing the work on the ground noted other problems. According to Inspector D.J. Martin:

It will be seen that none of the Eskimos in the Mackenzie Delta have discs. This fact, coupled

---

34 Roberts, *Eskimo Identification*, 16.

35 Roberts, *Eskimo Identification*, 16.

with the report that certain Eskimos on Boothia
Peninsula destroyed their discs after receiving them,
more or less throws the whole system of Eskimo
Identification out of line.[36]

Although it had already been suggested that the
"Eskimo will fall in line" with the memorization of their disc
number, the system had now "fallen out of line" through
the resistance of a few Inuit on the Boothia Peninsula and
others who had yet to receive a disc. Enforcing Canadian
state sovereignty in the North created unexpected and
unforeseen situations that troubled those in authority. As
the destruction of the discs shows, sovereignty sometimes
appears to be unmanageable.

The implementation of the disc system was off to a
rough start and to restore it from perceived disorder in 1943
all RCMP detachments were "instructed to submit, in triplicate to this office (Ottawa), a list of names of all Eskimos
who have been issued with identification discs to date, showing the number of the discs against each name."[37] McKeand
also asked that the lists be reworked from the 1941 census
up to and including 1945. Lists of disc numbers for newborn
babies were to be added into all disc lists. "Also, all lists
are to show the marital status, age and occupation of each
recipient and in the case of married women the number of

---

36   Cited in Roberts, *Eskimo Identification*, 17.

37   Roberts, *Eskimo Identification*, 17.

children she has had." Detachment officers were asked to make more copies in order to share this information with other detachments as "this would serve to keep a check on natives who move from one district to another."[38]

I had found another crack I could work at to find my grandmother. If the administration was collecting data on marital status and recording children, then maybe, just maybe, my grandmother would be among the names on one of those lists. But my hopes were dashed almost as quickly as I had resurrected them. Based on the instructions that McKeand issued, single Inuk moms and their children would not have been included on the lists. The influence of Christianity and the power of the sovereign was felt not only through the building of churches in the North and the presence of various religions and their leaders but also through who would be included on a list that was stored in Ottawa.

What happened if you were a single mom with three children, each of whom was issued a disc but was not included on the official lists stored in our country's capital? Were Inuk single mothers considered to be even more sub-human because they had not followed the Christian constructs of marriage? Were single Inuk moms without formal representation as community members because they were widows or had experienced a divorce? It is a form of punishment in the sense that personal circumstances surrounding a single mother are not taken into consideration and if she

---

38   Roberts, *Eskimo Identification*, 18.

is not on a disc list does that mean that the single Inuk mom does not exist?

My grandfather, Husky Harris, had three wives, one of them who happened to be my grandmother. The church did not condone polygamous relationships, and so their marriage would not have been recognized officially. This meant that my grandmother was considered a single mother and would not appear on the disc lists that had been created by the church. I had reached an end to this line of research: Those who created the Eskimo Identification Canada system had the power to decide who would be included and who would be excluded, even though those who created the system also created more confusion and more work for themselves through their constant revamping of the system. My grandmother was not on any of those lists.

The government, in an effort to assert authority over the North, became laden with paperwork and the writing of information in triplicate while exchanging disc list copies with one another. To ease the administrative burden, officials requested assistance with the paperwork but the response from Ottawa was that work needed to be organized "in such a manner as to carry it on with the existing staff of the Bureau of the Northwest Territories and Yukon Affairs because we cannot secure any additional help under war conditions."[39] In 1944 a new set of instructions was sent out into the field indicating that the Department of Vital

---

39   Roberts, *Eskimo Identification*, 20.

Statistics would now be handling the information. It came with the instruction that all disc information concerning newborn Inuit children be handled expediently and that discs from those who had passed away should be attached to death certificates and returned to Ottawa. Proof of both new life and of death revolve around a number that no one else in Canada had to report.

Having run into yet another dead end trying to track my grandmother through the disc lists, I dug deeper. I discovered that in 1945, the Canadian government instituted a Family Allowance, whereby each Canadian family was issued five dollars per child as a national social welfare program. W.F. Shepherd wrote to Major D.L. McKeand, noting that:

> To date no attempt has been made to enter on our Vital Statistics birth returns, completed prior to the 1941 census, the identification numbers which have since been issued to each Eskimo, nor has this been done on birth returns received since 1941, on which the identification number was omitted.[40]

In this instance, the system had been running for approximately four years but the information had not been recorded by the department. The department would have been consulted concerning the distribution of Family Allowance. The Inuit were issued store credits and not a

---

40   Qtd in Roberts, *Eskimo Identification*, 22.

cheque or cash,[41] and distribution would have been governed by who was on the disc list. This brings us back to the importance of being on a disc list: Would a single mother not be considered eligible for a national social welfare program? By 1970 the E-Number system was still in force and the Family Allowance benefit had increased to twenty dollars per child per month. In all those intervening years, would an Inuk mother and her children remain invisible to the state? State sovereignty presents strict rules and the sense of exclusion can run deep in the personal lives of Inuit mothers, but I felt a glimmer of hope: there was an outside chance my grandmother had made it onto the Family Allowance list.

No other Indigenous group had the money for the national Family Allowance program issued in store credits, an indication that perhaps Canada considered Inuit unable to manage money or commerce on their own. Issuing store credit also allowed for the continued surveillance of Inuit spending and made personal debt ratios accessible to government officials because Inuit were forced to spend in one store only. In this way, legislation, and the administration of that legislation, began to shrink freedom of movement for Inuit Canadians. But in this instance, this surveillance might just be the route through which I could enrol in the benefits program and enter my community.

---

41   Smith, "The Emergence of Eskimo Status," 45.

SANGUGIAQPAA – HE BEGINS TO CHANGE

In 1945 all the discs that were distributed, approximately 10,000, were recalled, new discs were struck, and the system began again. According to Smith,

> The stringent control required for the distribution of Family Allowances brought into being an effective registration program. The Arctic was divided into twelve districts West (W1, W2, W3) and East (E1 to E9). New disks were issued in blocks of numbers allocated to each district. The old disks recalled and replaced by new ones, small fibre disks free of design and stamped simply with a district designation and number, for example E3-1212.[42]

In 1945, state sovereignty over Inuit lands required tedious patience in order to achieve precision, as the recall and redistribution of the discs shows.

At approximately the same time and in conjunction with the disc system, residential schools were busy assimilating Inuit children. According to Sarah Bonesteel, "By the end of the Second World War, there were four residential schools and nine day schools in the Northwest Territories (NWT) and northern Quebec as well as several residential and day

---

42   Roberts, *Eskimo Identification*, 25.

schools in Labrador."[43] Education in the North had generally been provided in the form of mission schools and from the government's point of view there seemed little reason to do more. Again, it was a question of keeping the Natives Native:

> Why give Inuit children a white-oriented education when, for the foreseeable future, they would just be fur-trappers? Bureaucrats believed Inuit did not have the capacity to learn, that the "mental capacity to assimilate academic training is limited."[44]

As Richard Diubaldo notes in *A Historical Overview of Government-Inuit Relations, 1900–1980s*, "the onset of severe criticism by U.S. Army personnel and newspaper reporters over deplorable conditions amongst the Inuit"[45] in the Arctic was what compelled and pushed the Canadian government to review existing northern education practices as well as housing and continued death by starvation of the Inuit well into the 1950s.[46] Criticisms from United States' citizens stationed in Canada's North forced the Canadian state to examine and report on "the spotty and ineffectual education imparted by the missions, the acknowledged

---

43 Bonesteel, "The E-Number Identification System," 82.

44 Diubaldo, *A Historical Overview*, 91.

45 Diubaldo, *A Historical* Overview, 76.

46 Tester and Kuchylski, *Tammarniit*, 415.

intelligence of the Inuit, and the growing pace of change in a region entering the Cold War era."[47] It surprises me still that they saw what the Canadian government had not seen, or did not want to see.

Those who considered themselves rulers of the North of Canada now had outsiders looking in and sending reports to the U.S. president and Canadian government officials. The poverty and disparity that Inuit Canadians were living in was clearly on display and being reported to U.S. officials. The U.S. military reports pressured the Canadian government to begin making amends toward the Inuit, but many decades later and into the 2020s, food scarcity, poor housing, and an attrition rate of 59 per cent among Inuit high school students in Nunavut alone continue to remain as problems.[48] Eighty-plus years later and the Canadian state has yet to fully address basic human and educational needs of Inuit Canadians. The Canadian government is easily distracted and appears to only focus on Inuit-based problems when outsiders point them out.

---

47   Tester and Kuchylski, *Tammarniit*, 39.

48   Nunavut News. "Does Nunavut's Quality of Education Get a Passing Grade?" *Nunavut News*, March 29, 2020. https://www .nunavutnews.com/nunavut-news/does-nunavuts-quality -of-education-get-a-passing-grade/.

QUAQSITUQ — BEGINS TO FREEZE

On September 5, 1945, three days after the end of the Second World War and a month after the bombing of Hiroshima, a Soviet cipher clerk, Igor Sergeyevich Gouzenko, defected to the Canada with 109 documents detailing Soviet espionage activities in North America. Gouzenko's defection led to a renewed interest in the strategic importance of the Canadian North. Among the fallouts of Gouzenko's defection were the creation of North Atlantic Treaty Organization (NATO) at the start of the Cold War, and the building of the DEW Line. As Peter Pigott notes in *From Far and Wide: A History of Canada's Arctic Sovereignty*, the shortest distance between Siberia and the United States ran through the Canadian North, and with the lead-up to the Cold War that started in 1947, the Canadian North became the first line of defence against the Soviet Union and "the sovereignty of northern Canada was no longer of airbases, but its airspace."[49]

During the Second World War, the Canadian military had ramped up its presence in the North with a series of tactical manoeuvres, ending with Operation Lemming in March 1945. Planning began almost immediately for Operation Musk Ox in 1946. Operation Musk Ox involved a three-thousand-mile trip from Churchill, MB, to Grande Prairie, AB, with an estimated timeline of eighty days. The goal was to test the military's ability to move a small force

---

49   Pigott, *From Far and Wide*, 183.

overland in the Arctic; ultimately Operation Musk Ox proved that an overland invasion by the Soviet Union was unlikely. However, an aerial attack remained a concern. While all of this military movement and excess was occurring, some critics felt the Inuit were becoming too dependent on military bases as well as the radio stations set up in the North to maintain contact with the south. These stations, they noted, had become places that could provide food and the Inuit needed to return to their traditional ways of survival before contact with non-Inuit and before they relied too heavily on modern conveniences. They therefore proposed forced relocation of Inuit as the only option, publicly calling these relocations "voluntary migrations" that would help the Inuit make their return to self-reliance.[50]

Behind this propaganda lay a more strategic goal. Populated borders are a show of strategic sovereignty and moving Inuit along the coastal shores of the Hudson's Bay would be a critical display of ownership in the North.

My people are the Padlei or Ahiarmiut Inuit. On April 2, 1956, the front page of *Life* magazine displayed an Inuit man and woman looking upon a baby in its mother's arms—a very creche-like photo, with the caption underneath, "Stone Age Survivors: Eskimo Family."

The family are Ahiarmiut or Padlei Inuit, the Inuit deemed to be the last people in Canada to be influenced by non-Inuit. They were the last to move into modern-day

---

50   Marcus, *Relocating Eden*, 128.

existence as they lived inland and were farthest away from the settlements that were becoming small towns in northern Canada. Ennadai Lake is their original home territory and in May 1950 the state "relocated forty-seven people by air to Nueltin Lake, sixty miles (one hundred kilometres) to the southeast, where it was hoped they might work for a proposed commercial fishery scheme. The project failed and within a matter of months the Inuit found their way back home."[51] These relocated Inuit had walked the one hundred kilometres home. Several died of starvation on that walk.

In 1955–56 the caribou did not follow the usual migratory pattern and the Inuit began to starve. They were considered a burden to the government radio station that had been established at Ennadai. The state intervened again because these circumstances and decreed "that the status quo should come to an abrupt end, and that action should once again be taken to relocate the Ahiarmiut away from the vicinity of the radio station...this time they would have to be moved farther afield to prevent a replay of the earlier imbroglio at Nueltin Lake."[52] With much fanfare and a press release titled, "Eskimos Fly to New Hunting Grounds," a total of fifty-nine Padlei Inuit and their six dogs were moved to Henik Lake, a place of forced relocation.

They were the only people in the area. The nearest outpost was three days away and the Inuit thought "they had

51   Marcus, *Relocating Eden*, 194.

52   Marcus, *Relocating Eden*, 195.

been sent away" and were being punished. "Within eight months, eight members of this small group were dead. Dead from starvation. Dead from desperation. Dead from exposure. Dead from neglect and from not having lived up to the popular, pictorially, informed stereotype."[53] After this failed relocation attempt, after the starvation deaths of eight Padlei Inuit, my people were flown into Tikirarjuaq, NU, in 1958.

It is in this year that all relocation programs of the Inuit were stopped. David Serkoak, who has been mentioned already, is a living member of all the relocations coerced upon the Padlei or Ahiarmiut Inuit. It is Serkoak who spent twenty years fighting for and finally achieving an apology from the Canadian government in 2018. Sixty years later, survivors of the Padlei relocations and their children were recognized. The settlement for the surviving Inuit equalled $5 million. A memorial plaque listing those who were lost during the relocations was unveiled in Arviat.[54]

The Eastern Arctic Inuit had also experienced several relocations along with the slaughtering of thousands of their dog teams. It was thought that without the dog teams the

---

53   Marcus, *Relocating Eden*, 196.

54   Malbeuf, Jamie. "Ahiarmiut and Federal Gov't Reach $5M Settlement for Relocations." *CBC News*. August 27, 2018. https://www.cbc.ca/news/canada/north/ahiarmiut-settlement-ennadai-lake-1.4800781.

Inuit in the east would stay put.[55] They were wrong. Sadly, as the Qikiqtani Truth Commission reports make very clear, these relocation examples show that those who claimed sovereign power over the Inuit made decisions that resulted in many Inuit deaths. It only took the Canadian government six decades to acknowledge their own wrongdoing.

UIRITTUQ — BEGINS TO HAVE HABIT OF DOING SOMETHING THAT PLEASES

In the midst of all of this upheaval the Inuit remained a numerically marked group of people and it was not until 1966, the silver anniversary of the disc system, that the commissioner of the Northwest Territories brought the issue to the administrator of the Arctic, asking:

It seems to me that there is only one justification for assigning a number to people

> and actually putting it on a disc. That is, if an absolute requirement exists for identifying people and the alternatives would be an unacceptable level of confusion. It strikes me that we should discontinue the number system and the disc system as soon as possible.[56]

---

55   QIA, *Qimmiliriniq*, 39.

56   Roberts, *Eskimo Identification*, 26.

This administrator refused this suggestion because Inuit in some settlements had adopted surnames already. In some areas, the administrator noted, government officials "have run into the problem of a number of people from one settlement with the same Christian name and surname who are approximately the same age. When there are three Annie Kilauks living at Pangnirtung, NWT, the only positive means of identification is the identification number."[57]

When three Inuit women each take the name of Annie Kilauk, I see this as an intentional and subtle way to rebel against the non-Inuit. These women could state that they may not have known better because the non-Inuit never instructed them otherwise, but I suspect they were aware of what they were doing. It is in effect a funny prank and inside of that prank is a strong sense of resistance. This form of resistance on the part of the Inuit is humour-filled and one must wonder who truly is holding the sovereignty baton.

In 1968 the dissolution of the disc system reached the NWT Council chamber. However, it was not until mid-1971 that the first steps were taken to replace the disc system with a new method of state control, Project Surname. The quest for state sovereign control of Inuit names ended and through it all, as Inuit, we survived and thrived and continue into present day. As Mary Simon, currently the first female Inuk Governor General (appointed in 2021) and former Inuit national leader, stated in a 2011 paper, "Inuit are

---

57   Roberts, *Eskimo Identification*, 27.

a patient and practical people. We know that the economic and social problems that we face did not come about overnight, and will not be remedied overnight. We know that most of these problems are problems of history and circumstance, not prejudice or bad intentions."[58] In saying this, Simon reinforced that Inuit are survivors and a force to be dealt with not only on a national but also an international level and as survivors we continue into present day.

For someone like me, who was looking to prove my connection to my ancestral home, the disc system had meant a loss of traditional naming practices and an inability to trace my grandmother. It is not only those who were given disc numbers who suffered, but also those who did not, and their descendants.

---

58   Simon, "Canadian Inuit," 888.

kinaugavit?

(Can I get your name?)

> When a child is born it is the parents or in-laws who name the child. The spirit of a relative or best friend, who has just died will be born again in the new baby by their name, and we then call out that name when the mother is birthing.[1]

In my search for my grandmother, I learned much about traditional naming practices and began to understand what we had lost under state sovereignty and with the disc system. The naming of a child for Inuit is ceremonial. In the epigram for this chapter, we see that the entrance into the world of an Inuk newborn is not a process experienced solely between mother and child. The name of the child is chanted by those who surround the mother as the labour persists. The name the child will carry is in remembrance and honour of a relative or friend. That name is sung to the child as they are arriving into the world. A name is the most important item that an Inuk child will carry.

---

1   Crnkowvic, *Gossip*, 117.

I birthed four sons into the world and upon the arrival of each of my little boys, I would phone my mom and ask her if the name I wanted to give them was okay with her. She did ask why I wanted that particular name and then would say, "Yes," after I explained my reasoning to her. For me it was a part of the process of naming my sons. My mom's approval mattered. It was important for me that she liked the names of each of my sons and what they represented. Inuit tradition does not die off entirely.

Expectant parents spend a great deal of time wrestling with the name that their child will carry. In western thinking, many parents honour their ancestors by naming a child after someone who may have recently passed on. However, the Inuit naming system extends the name into the spiritual realm, meaning that child will be apprenticed in all skills and characteristics of the person after whom they were named. Carrying someone's name means becoming the good characteristics of that person. In *We Call It Survival: The Life Story of Abraham Okpik*, Abe Okpik describes this kind of kinship that arises from naming a child after someone who has left this physical world. He speaks of naming the Inuit child after that person and then raising them with the skills and personality that that person had. Okpik speaks of the drum that is played when the newborn arrives and the chants and dancing that accompany the happy event. He called this kind of arrival in the world "a song of love" and it is just that. Okpik presents the beauty of naming within Inuit tradition and how those who we love stay with us.[2] How their soul takes up residence within the next generation who are taught to carry the traits and skills of their namesake. Through his retelling of his own namesake's story, Okpik connects the tradition of a happy song to the word "atuvalluk" and reminds us of the love that binds tradition from one generation to the next. He describes how Inuit naming is a purposeful yet tender process and how leaving a song of love is important.

His recollection and sharing of the Inuit naming system lies very much in opposition to the Eskimo Identification Canada system that initially was birthed onto the tundra by non-Inuit administrators who had problems pronouncing and spelling Inuit names. Instead of taking the time to learn how to say and spell an Inuk name by conversing with the Inuit themselves, the government of the day removed Inuit names and replaced them with a numbering system that amounted to an early form of digital surveillance.

The only government-supplied document that is exclusive to the Eskimo Identification system was prepared by A. Barry Roberts in 1975. In his report for the Social Development division, Department of Indian and Northern Affairs, he wrote that the confusion of Inuit names lay firstly with the missionaries. Non-Inuit see and hear confusion while Inuit hear incantations of songs containing love and songs that brought happiness through an Inuk's name. Roberts indicates that as early as 1933 the government of

---

2   Okpik, *We Call it Survival,* 54.

Canada was looking for a method that would standardize the spelling of Inuit names and he notes that "the department (Department of the Interior NWT) should adopt some universal form of identification of the Eskimo population."[3]

Eskimo Identification and Disc Numbers: A Brief History contains sessional documents and lengthy extracts of the historic exchanges between the Northwest Territory government employees between 1933 and 1968. Roberts presents an edited and possibly altered version of the written communications between government officials. When I started doing my research into Inuit naming practices and the disc system, I often thought of A. Barry Roberts and wondered how much he was allowed to include on behalf of the state. Were there documents that were censored and redacted to a point of no understanding? What portions of these historic letters between those who contrived the system were given approval to be made public? And by whom? The documents do not show any interaction with the Inuit. Never once are the Inuit consulted for their view of the implementation of the system. Never once are the Inuit asked for their opinion of the ujamit or their necklace identifiers.

Roberts presents a document that is government-quote heavy. He writes little of his own words aside from the introductory pages. He is providing evidence of a system that has yet to be recognized and based, I assume, on what he cannot freely write about as he is writing on behalf of the federal

---

3   Roberts, *Eskimo Identification*, 3.

government. What Roberts does well through the use of these quotes is to allow the reader to gain an understanding of the tone of the government's thoughts and processes. Roberts allows us to see why the system was so important to the government.

This document introduces the reader to "Project Surname," the by-product of the disc system. This program gave Inuit last names and was followed by "Project Correction."[4] Project Correction was the third government-initiated venture into organizing Inuit naming. After introducing Project Surname, Ottawa soon recognized that family members within the same household had chosen different last names, which confused the federal government. This third adventure into Inuit naming had each member of the same household change their last name to the same name. Roberts provides the historic background to the Eskimo Identification Canada system and the non-Inuit understanding of the need for the system. For historic purposes, this text does have value in terms of what was happening on the government side of things.

When I read Roberts' work, I think about how as human beings we have the ability to justify our actions no matter how right or wrong our actions are. This sense of reasoning is innate. It is human nature to be able to take the most outrageous actions and yet we can tell ourselves and others that our actions were necessary during that time or at that place.

---

4   Alia, *Names & Nunavut Culture*, 115.

This does not mean that I am sympathetic toward the federal government of the day or at any time, but it does mean that I understand the government felt they had a quick solution to a growing problem. That problem, however, was their own laziness: despite the volumes of reports and directives, they could not find time to spend with the Inuit, the people they felt compelled to control.

The next government-sponsored document that refers to Inuit was released on July 30, 1992, and titled, *A Historical Overview of Government-Inuit Relations, 1900–1980s*. It was written by Richard J. Diubaldo, a university professor and historian. This document was released by the Department of History, Concordia University, Montreal, and is in effect a fulfillment of a request from the government to various scholars throughout Canada. This document is a preview on Indigenous Canadian groups prior to the report presented by the Royal Commission on Aboriginal People (RCAP) to Parliament in November of 1996.

In the entire document, there is not one reference made to the Eskimo Identification Canada system. I was searching for information I could use to help me trace my ancestors, and I knew the disc system lay at the heart of my own difficulties in being enrolled in the benefit program. I could not believe that the Eskimo Identification system did not warrant even a mention since the document covers the entire period from the early 1700s history into 1988 northern policymaking in Canada's Arctic. Allowing Diubaldo, the chosen academic historical writer, to omit any reference to the disc system is baffling. It is most unsettling. How could a system that became entrenched not only within Inuit society but also within the workings and minds of non-Inuit administrators be disregarded so blatantly? The reasoning behind the decision to exclude the disc system may have been that the system was officially disbanded at the time of RCAP. However, this was a historical study requested by the government, and it should have mentioned a system that lay central to Inuit identification. I was shocked when I realized that the disc system did not bear mentioning to the most important committee reviewing the state of Inuit Canadians. I was insulted as a researcher, and as an Inuk, to discover that Diubaldo had made such a huge oversight.

Seventeen years after the publication of Roberts' work, the disc or E-Number system appeared to have vanished from official record. The system may have been omitted based on the many appellations it had held—disc system, disk system, or E-Number system—or it may be an example of how this invasive system had become normalized by both Inuit and non-Inuit. It may also have been too shameful for the government to admit to having implemented it. Yet here I found myself and my people written out of history yet again. In a report that was being used on a national scale, the effects of the system were not heard. Inuk stories about the disc system were not spoken or recorded in what would have been one of the most power-filled documents presented to the government of Canada on behalf of Inuit Canadians.

Stories like those of John Arnalukjuak and Rachel Uyarasuk are absent.

John Arnalukjuak, in a 1997 interview, states, "We were told by the RCMP not to lose those discs so we were fearful that, uh, if we ever lose them, because that, in those days, the RCMP were really bossy and you know, so we feared them. So, we were told not to lose them." Rachel Uyarasuk did lose all her family's discs. "I was afraid to lose mine...We were told not to lose them...I didn't wear it around my neck. All my children's and mine...I tied them together. And I lost them! I was ever scared." Uyarasuk realized her family's discs were lost while they were travelling from one winter camp to another. The family returned to their first camp and "even picked on the ice, looking for them...I had to tell someone because we had lost them, and I was very scared. I thought I was going to be arrested."[5]

John Arnalukjuak's experience shows how the government used coercion, force, and threats to implement and maintain the system. The red coats were heavily armed with authority and described as bullies who created fear for an Inuk male. Panic and trepidation filled Rachel Uyarasuk to the point that she returned to a dismantled camp and tried to break up the ice in search of her family's discs because she feared being sent to jail for the human act of losing an item.

What I see is how a small disc encompassed complete control and fear over Inuit Canadians and how the heavy

---

5   Tester and Kulchyski, *Kiumajut*, 98.

hand of a police force, a group that is mandated to protect citizens, can abuse their power. To have an Inuk mom say, "I was very scared. I thought I was going to be arrested," indicates the horror that filled her. How can losing your family's discs result in jail time? I have not been able to find a law designed specifically to punish Inuit who misplaced their necklaces, so the fear that Rachel had has to be a demonstration of the coercive control that those in authority carried over the Inuit. It also shows how the everyday movements, the daily processes of living and going about a day, were controlled by the possession of a tiny, numbered disc.

Surveillance does not need to depend on high-powered cameras. When the free flow of everyday living is controlled by the possession of a numbered necklace, there is something wrong happening. When an entire system of control is not included in a written government-sponsored narrative, there is a large gap in information. When the voices of those most affected are not a part of any historic document are we, as Canadian citizens, not being censored and written out of the history the government allows us to access?

Although Diubaldo completely bypassed the disc system, what he did provide is a critical rendering of the government's attitude toward the Inuit at that time. Under the sub-heading of Inuit Legal Status, he states,

To this day, Inuit are considered ordinary citizens of Canada, without any special legal status. In the mid-1980s, officials of the Department of Indian Affairs and Northern Development, when queried, could only say that "[t]here is no federal statute which provides for a defined 'legal' Inuit status. Inuit 'status' is a matter of combined community and self-identification based on cultural, ancestral, or racial criteria and possibly territorial factors."[6]

In relation to the disc system, this statement can provide a peek into how the Canadian government had at one time viewed the Inuit as a task to be undertaken not with bravado but with brevity. There is not another group of Indigenous Canadians who were without treaty or a lands claim at the time, or who had been given a disc number to be handled in the most unceremonious of manners. With little to no fanfare the federal government of Canada managed to eliminate the use of Inuit names. Overall,

The Canadian government demonstrated its reluctance to tackle the social and legal problems in other than the old-style colonial approach, with its attendant yet subtle racism...concern for the welfare of the Inuit was always present but never paramount.[7]

Diubaldo's report did show the RCAP committee the begrudging attitude that persisted with the Canadian

---

6   Diubaldo, *A Historical Overview*, 10.

7   Diubaldo, *A Historical Overview*, 11.

government and that lack of enthusiasm and care toward Inuit remains commonplace in present-day. Inuit remain nothing more than an item of reluctance.

UQALIQTUQAQTUQ – SPEAKS QUICKLY, HURRYING

A more recent publication by Sarah Bonesteel released by Indian and Northern Affairs Canada in June of 2006 and pages 37–39 are set aside for the Eskimo Identification Canada system in what is titled, *The E-Number Identification System*, a text of less than two thousand words.

Bonesteel, like Roberts, begins with a brief explanation of the traditional Inuit naming system, bringing to light the struggle that non-Inuit missionaries, whalers, traders, and RCMP had in their basic dealings with Inuit when they invaded the North under the guise of offering social benefits, commerce, and education. She mentions the confusion among Hudson's Bay Company employees and medical doctors experienced with Inuit names and mentions the fingerprinting of Inuit in the 1930s. I had to wonder how the Inuit in 1930 made this association. How did they associate fingerprinting with breaking the law or was it the very fact that a trip to the doctor now included being fingerprinted by the RCMP who were present at the medical office? Attending to a physical need should not be equated with criminality. Medical doctors are not enforcers of western law and their role is to aid the patient, not fingerprint them. Bonesteel references the statement by Dr J.A. Bildfell who noted that the Inuit were frightened by the process of fingerprinting and Inuit traditional legal systems would not have included putting inked prints onto a page or sitting in a jail cell. How foreign the concept of western law must have been to Inuit even in the early 1940s in Canada's North.

Bonesteel does note how "all Inuit interaction with the federal and provincial or territorial governments required use of E-numbers,"[8] but what she neglects to mention is that officials deliberately refused food, medicine, social services, or any type of government-based aid to the Inuit if they did not have an E-Number next to their name in a trading post book or other tracking mechanism, or on their person. These same government services were expected and extended to all other non-Inuit Canadians who were never issued a disc number.

Bonesteel writes that the system was terminated because over time the government came to rationalize that "alphanumeric registration of Inuit as a primary means of identification...was uncommon for other cultural groups in Canada." The fact that this system ran for a minimum of thirty to thirty-four years is not mentioned. Project Surname, a program that continued the decimation of traditional naming systems, is mentioned only once, in the closing line of Bonesteel's report: "Currently, Inuit are known by given names and surnames, and are registered

---

8   Bonesteel, "The E-Number Identification System," 39.

through vital statistics records, as are people throughout the rest of Canada."[9]

The last eight words sting. Bonesteel suggests that Inuit are now like all other Canadians. Nothing could be further from the truth: it is as though through a colonial act the justification for the removal of traditional names, systems of birth and death, the ceremony that is attached to the entrance and exiting of this world, is not worthy of mention. To think that we, as Inuit, wanted to be transformed into the likeness of all other Canadians and at long last are finally on par is a paternalistic and highly colonial point of view. Inuit, like other cultures, remain distinct and are far more than a number.

I have taught a required Indigenous Canadian history and present-day circumstance course in the Faculty of Education at the University of Alberta since 2015. I present the content of the course a little differently each semester, but the basics of the course remain in place. I also spend ninety-minutes lecturing on the Eskimo Identification Canada system. My students are often stunned that this system existed in Canada, and they have somehow managed to live over twenty years of their lives without knowing about it. They are angered that Canada has lied to them by omitting the history of Inuit within their education. They are insulted that they had to sit in a second-year university class to learn about something that should have been taught when they were in high school.

---

9   Bonesteel, "The E-Number Identification System," 39.

Over the length of the course, they begin to see how Canada has intentionally omitted information and they are saddened to realize what the truth is about Inuit. They ask me why they weren't told anything about the disc system. I remind them that curriculum is decided mainly by the province but when I review the documents in the library, online, or in the archives, the reality is that there is not much information available. If something is kept out of sight, in this case information about an Inuit-specific government-contrived system, then it falls to reason that the same information will be kept from the public. Canada enjoys being the good guys on the world stage and would never allow one blemish to be placed on that reputation, so why would this type of information be included in the K–12 system of any school in Canada? The only Inuk male to write anything on the system was Zebedee Nungak, an Inuk politician:

> The disk number has a special significance in our lives, even with the abundance of identifications we carry today. Every Eskimo once committed his or her E-Number to memory, a handy ID for all purposes. One of a mother's great duties was keeping track of all her family's E-numbers. Even in this age of email-dot-com, I know many who still use their *ujamik* numbers as a PIN for charge cards, a house number, or a label for their belongings. Losing my disk in

early childhood has never erased the number that
was so much a part of my early life.[10]

Zebedee, in his humorous and sarcastic way, confesses
how the loss of his original necklace did not wipe clean his
number from his memory. We each carry numeric codes
within our memories now. These codes are requirements
within our own daily electronic lives, but they are numeric
codes of our own design and not government-issued. For
example, the PIN number to access our bank accounts is
one that is committed to our memories by choice not as a
mandate from the federal government.

We are people creating passwords that are not a
requirement to the fulfillment of the basic needs of life. Our
passwords are not a government requirement needed to
indicate where we live, what we ate through our purchases
at a store, whether we attended school, what our medical
ailments are, or how much money we earned. Inuit children
were less than kindergarten age when they memorized their
E-numbers. How does a government-imposed number affect
the carefree existence of a child? How does oppression and
the sense of being "bad" affect an Inuit child when they don't
know their number at school at the age of five? What kind
of trauma or harm results and resides inside a childhood
memory because at the local store they forgot their number

---

10   Nungak, "E9–1956," 37.

when buying candy? Non-Inuit Canadian children would not have experienced the weight of a government-assigned number nor the infringement on their liberty that comes with it.

What the Canadian state never admits to or takes ownership of is how the disc system damaged the younger Inuit generations and how this damage was heaped upon young children. Canadian society must think beyond the practical mechanics of running a system that only conveniences those not affected. Consider how Nungak tells of the maternal responsibility of each Inuk mom and the importance of keeping track of numbers for all of their family members, an additional pressure to child-rearing. It now becomes the responsibility of the Inuk mom to make sure that each child has memorized their E-Number. That same Inuk mom would have to explain the importance that the number held and how that number allowed them access to the basics of life, including the pleasure of putting a candy into their mouth. This is something that revolts me as an Inuk and as a citizen of Canada.

It is Major McKeand who first wrote about the importance of memorizing the assigned number:

> In my opinion there is no necessity whatsoever for replacing the present identification disk with a medal or token of any kind. As I have been pointing out for twenty years, **once the Eskimo realizes that the white man wants him to memorize an identification number and use it in all trading and other**

transactions, the Eskimo will fall in line. There will be no need for the Eskimo to wear identification disks for a longer period than is required for him and his family and friends to memorize the number (emphasis added).[11]

What McKeand requires is obedience and submission. Those thirty words sum up the attitude of the white man toward the Eskimo: one of superiority, master versus servant.

I had hoped with each government-issued publication that the voice of the Inuit would at last be released in print. It was not. I had hoped that Inuit voices would speak of the felt and lived meaning of a disc number, as a part of everyday business, whether at a doctor's office or in a classroom. They were not given that chance in any of the reports I have read. I had hoped that a rendering of how a disc number became a form of not only Inuit identity, but of authenticity, would also be placed into print. It was not.

The fact that Inuit have always been more than a number and the effects of a numbered necklace as a form of validation of existence is not given any thought. Zebeedee Nungak writes, "Then the system choked and sputtered to a demise unworthy of a brilliant government idea. It was never officially retired, nor its end duly marked by an appropriate solemn ceremony presided over by Inuit."[12]

---

11   Roberts, *Eskimo Identification*, 23.

12   Nungak, "E9–1956," 37.

Nungak is in his own way again poking fun at a system that did not receive a proper burial. Dying at the age of thirty years is something that should have been noteworthy in some form but since the system never received a birth announcement perhaps an obituary was not required either. When I was researching the Eskimo Identification Canada system, I often reflected on how the white administrators saw the system as something that was harmless, something that was a quick and semi-permanent fix to *their* problems. I would think about how even today many people continue that type of thinking. After all, a number alone did not lead to loss of life; a number did not produce bodily scars that could be shown; and Inuit did not seem to complain.

The longevity of the system can be seen as an indicator of its success from a government perspective. Between 1941 and 1971, a total of five prime ministers, four of whom are leaders of the Liberal Party, oversaw governance of our country, and that included applying the Eskimo Identification Canada system. I have often thought of how not one of them saw the wrong that lay in the system, that not one of them called a halt to it. That not one of them thought that the only Indigenous group in Canada to be tagged and numbered were citizens of their country or that the system was counterintuitive to the image of Canada overall.

As a child, I thought of these prime ministers as good men with good morals. Men who embraced Canada as a country that was vast and free and open to all who wanted to come and live here. Men who in my growing up years were spoken about by my folks as men who provided a sense of security and wholesomeness to us as citizens. Research allows a great deal of time for personal reflection.

When Indigenous researchers are investigating our pasts, we are mainly looking inward at ourselves or our own Indigenous family and friends. I have read enough on non-Inuit and their reasoning and justifications of the disc system. It is time for the voice of the Inuit to appear and sing as loud as it can. It is time.

imngiqtuq

(She sings)

Not all scars lie on the outside of our bodies. Many are not visible and lie deep inside our spirits. I hold the advantage of being well-educated and I was given the opportunity of time to investigate that one question, "What was your mother's disc number?" This is the question that sparked this book but also a question that kindled a song released by Inuk artist Tatanniq Lucie Idlout. Her song, "E5-770 My Mother's Name," was released in 2003. Idlout lets loose onto the world her absolute disgust toward the disc system and those who numbered her mom. She does not hold back and in her own way brings satire and small bits of humour to her song.

Lucie's mother, Leah Idlout, passed away in 2005. Leah was a renowned Elder, educator and writer, and a trailblazer on behalf of Inuit women through Pauktuutit Inuit Women of Canada and the Inuit Non-Profit Housing Association and Lucie's song is a tribute to a remarkable woman. "E5-770" makes use of an Inuit traditional song type, the iviutit. Iviutit songs "were used to embarrass people, to make fun of them, to make fun of their weaknesses."[1] An iviutit song

---

1   Aupilaarjuk "Pisiit, Songs," 201.

battle was a legal and binding method of maintaining peace and order within Inuit groupings. It was a way of stopping physical revenge.[2] Inuit used song over fists. Through her song, Idlout rightly leaves a stain of embarrassment on the country of Canada and rightly throws into the faces of the authorities a system that treated Inuit as less than human.

Her repetitive use of the words that form the chorus, "You farmed my mother E5-770. You imposed your name number," clearly connects to Idlout's further descriptions of Inuit being treated like cattle and how the disc system was a form of branding. In an email response to me, Idlout said that she wrote this song because she "hated the idea of her mother being referred to by anything other than her proper name" and she "wanted to expose the country (meaning Canada) because at the time the song was written Canada was rated as one of the top countries in the world to live in."[3] Idlout thought this was "a fucking joke considering how many treaties have been broken and how many Aboriginal peoples live in poverty." She concludes, "I wrote it in the style I did to make people listen to a voice that is rarely heard or recognized, and issues that are rarely spoken or acknowledged in a spoken form. Music makes people hear you."[4]

What Idlout says is really important: the Inuit voice is rarely heard or recognized. In having no voice Inuit are not

---

2   Aupilaarjuk, "Pisiit, Songs," 201–219.

3   Personal communication, Oct 24, 2011.

4   Personal communication, Oct 24, 2011.

heard in the same manner as non-Inuit. When she writes, "Music makes people hear you," she is talking about how music can reach people in a way that a lecture or speech can not. Idlout sang this song with her band in several venues across Canada and I asked her how the audience reacted. She told me that people would dance to it, but I hope, too, that she may have placed into the non-Inuit conscience an exposure to a system that Canada has yet to discuss.

Susan Aglukark is a highly awarded Inuk. She has performed for many politicians and has received countless accolades, yet she remains humble. She is a song writer, singer, and author who released her own song, "E186" in 1999. It is not an assigned number, but like Lucie Idlout, Susan uses traditional Inuit musical forms to convey her message. It is a soft song of resistance, and it reflects the traditional type of Inuit song known as a pisiq. A pisiq "tells of things that happened in the past" and are "sung with a drum" as the dominant instrument.[5] Her song is sung in a much softer tone and the words are impactful. She sings how "you can not wipe away what is written in the soul" and she acknowledges that the removal of Inuit names through a number was a lasting kind of hurt. Aglukark is singing of and to the heroes who survived a system that tried to

---

5   David Owingayak, "David Owingayak," interview by Solomon Kugak, *Inuktitut Magazine*, no. 54. Ottawa: *Indian and Northern Affairs*, 1984.

remove names and cultural identity and, in many ways, tried to erase the faces of the Inuit.

Each of these amazing artists brings into play the Inuit value system known as Inuit Qaujimajatuqangit. Translated into English those two words mean "that which Inuit have long known" and it is the way that Inuit are born into the world, and it is within this value system they are raised. It involves the concept of blood memory and how our ancestors pass onto us their own understandings and memories. As Inuit and as Indigenous Canadians we have to recognize that not all of the memories of our ancestors were bad memories, and we are still standing when in theory we should not be. Inuit Qaujimajatuqangit (IQ) is a part of how every Inuk is, and it lies inside us waiting to be put to use.

Inuit Qaujimajatuqangit are the Inuit values and ways of knowing and being.[6] IQ can be used to understand how Inuit thought of the Eskimo Identification Canada system. The following are a few of the values:

Inuuqatigiitsiarniq—showing respect and caring for one another. When we work together, we build relationships that matter. When the non-Inuit came into the Arctic and started to remove Inuit names and replaced names with a

---

6   Morgan Bentham, "Guiding Principles and Values of Inuit Qaujimajatuqangit (IQ)," Teacher as Researcher, 2016. https://leapintothevoidwithme.wordpress.com/2016/04/09/principles-of-inuit-qaujimajatuqangit/#more-314.

number, Inuit appeared to have been in agreement because we did not outwardly fight back. That attitude does not lie within Inuit. It is more important to be respectful toward those who do not understand us and if what the white man wanted was to have a numbered necklace to be on our person—who would that hurt?

Tunnganarniq—being welcoming to others. Ajua Peter explained the welcoming to shore of those who did not look like Inuit and I have spoken many times about my mom taking care of people who came into our home no matter the time of day or night. Being welcoming is essential to Inuit because we can not turn people away. All of our relationships should be positive. Inuit would have never turned the non-Inuit administrators away from their homes.

Piliriqatigiingniq—working together for a common purpose or consensus. For Inuit, working together is not about forcing anyone into doing something or changing their mind but about reaching a common goal on which everyone agreed. If the non-Inuit wanted to try to understand the Inuit through the use of a number, then so be it. An Inuk Elder once said to me, "We just wore them for the government," meaning that if this is what helped the government people, then Inuit helped.

Qanuqtuurunnarniq—being resourceful to solve problems. Inuit would have recognized that the non-Inuit had a problem. They did not understand Inuit names. Therefore if wearing a necklace with a number on it helped non-Inuit then the problem would be solved. I think this demonstrates how Inuit were firstly not aggressive and secondly not self-seeking.

Pijitsirniq—the concept of serving. Idlout and Aglukark each served their people by writing and putting onto the airwaves songs that spoke of the Eskimo Identification Canada system. Inuit will always serve one another and also serve those who are non-Inuit. This is a part of how we function in the world. Life is not about self. Life is about others.

When the values are added up and the wonderful qualities that Inuit adhere to are taken into consideration it becomes clearer to see how Inuit may have welcomed non-Inuit. They would have helped them to understand the tundra environment. How to handle the cold. How to hunt the local wildlife. What to do with animal hides and skins. How to piece together clothing to keep warm. How to store food.

What Inuit would not have expected was the interference that resulted later. The intrusive barging in and taking over of their daily lives by non-Inuit and the constant oppression.

iqqaumavit?

(Do you remember?)

Inuit names suffered butchery from the pens of Qallunaat who could never finesse the phonetics of the Inuktitut language...In such cases, an individual's E-Number was a basic confusion-saver...Statistical specifics were not a particular preoccupation of Inuit. Slack inaccuracy in records was the norm, and Inuit were quite indifferent to such sloppiness...Inuit responses to Qallunaat questions about such statistics were classic and legendary in their innocent honesty, "How old are you?" "I don't know." "When were you born?" "In the spring just as the geese were arriving."—or "In the fall two days after the first snowfall." One can just see the recorder putting down: "Age: 45, born 1902" by just taking another look at his subject. But then who needed accuracy? Would an Eskimo ever need a passport, or apply for employment insurance?"[1]

---

1   Nungak, "E9-1956," 34.

I could not have completed this work without the participation from the Inuit in this chapter. I can never put into words or thank each of them enough for having shared their honest and wonder-filled stories. Their lives speak of strength and courage.

ALAN VOISEY, TIKIRARJUAQ (WHALE COVE), NU
Date: September 19, 2013

Alan Voisey is a volunteer participant in the truest sense. On September 13, 2013, Northern News Services editor Darrell Greer ran a story titled, "Raising their Voices, Master's Student looking for ID tag experiences in Kivalliq."[2] I had emailed asking for advertising space to make a request for interviewees to come forward. Mr. Greer answered my request by writing and printing a full, front-page story in the *Kivalliq News*, the weekly newspaper distributed in the Tikirarjuaq area.[3] Five nights later Alan Voisey called my home.

In my first conversation with Alan we talked over our kinship ties. His brother Lewis may possibly be a distant relation of mine and this connection is made through the

---

2   Darrell Greer, "Raising their Voices, Master's Student looking for ID tag experiences in Kivalliq," Northern News Services, On September 13, 2013.

3   Greer, "Raising their Voices."

marriage of my Auntie Frances to Johnny Voisey. What I had never known was that Lewis had a brother. Meeting Alan over the phone was an absolute delight for me.

Alan explains in our conversation that "Lewis was my mom's real son anyway and I was adopted" and he goes on to say, "I call him my big brother anyways and we do this and that, we go out and hunt, go out on machine, work on outboards." Adoption was a common practice in the North, free of social workers and documents. Elders Naqi Ekho and Uqsuralik Ottokie each spoke of how adoption was a normal part of Inuit life. Adoption was decided through the consensus of the entire community and children could move in with other families for a period of time whether that child was parentless or taken from their biological parents. The point here is that the process was communal, and the primary concern was what benefited the child most.[4]

Children are treasures for Inuit and belong to everyone within the community. The environment that they are raised in must be one of nurturing and trust. According to the explanation given by Elder Uqsuralik Ottokie, Alan would have become a community responsibility. Alan was an adopted child and given a home of trust and care through his adopted mother and family. His adoption is an example of tiguaq (adopted child).

Our first conversation was designed for each of us to figure out how we fell into the same family tree and to talk

---

4   Ekho and Ottokie, *Childrearing Practices*, 91–101.

over our cousins and various people in Tikirarjuaq, NU, and Churchill, MB. In other words, we gossiped! It was fun. We agreed to speak again the following evening but bad weather in Tikirarjuaq hampered connecting with each other at the designated time. Approximately two hours later we were able to connect, and Alan explained that he had to help Lewis with a boat as it was snowing and, in his words, a "grey and foggy today." In other words, normal northern weather in mid-September.

Alan Voisey at that time of our talk was a 51-year-old and a life-long resident of Tikirarjuaq. He was born on December 17, 1963. I ask him if his birth certificate has his disc number on it. He tells me he has to get his wallet and "his magnifying glass," a reference to his poor eyesight. There is no disc number on his birth certificate, but he tells me it was issued on March 12, 1964, almost three months after his birth. This fact may demonstrate the slowness of administration in the Arctic. It may also reflect on the fact that government-issued documents do not bear the import-ance that non-Indigenous peoples may place on them or their need to have identification documents with them at all times. I say this in remembrance of my mom, who never had an official birth certificate. She still managed to live a life without government documentation.

Alan is employed by Tikirarjuaq, a hamlet of 465 people. He is the person who delivers fuel to the homes of residents and laughs as he tells me he does this so he "doesn't have to hear their teeth rattling at night!" He is easy to speak with and filled with humour.

Alan says that he was introduced to his disc number, E1-856, at the age of eight. His adopted anaana (mother), Rosie Jessie Voisey, took the necklace out of a kitchen cupboard and told him that this was his number and that it was a part of Eskimo identification. Alan still has his stringed identifier. To his recollection he never had to make use of his number in any form. He says, "It never bothered me anyway."

As our conversation continues Alan makes mention of E2 people within a community that the government-designed borders had designated for E1 people. He remarks on the difference between E1 and E2 people:

> I've heard about a couple of people that they were
> E2 and they ask me if I had one too and when some-
> thing is memorized...you don't forget that number.
> It didn't matter to me, but older people than me, I
> heard them tell about it and they said they were
> mad and they say they don't need that kinda num-
> ber anyway...I don't know how they think about it. It
> didn't bother me.

Inuit prior to the disc system were a people without borders. The Eskimo Identification Canada system created unseen geographical perimeters akin to jail cells. It also placed into the Inuit conscious a non-Inuit form of identification, one that never originated with the Inuit. The disc system had invaded the Inuit psyche and Alan makes a point of distinguishing E1 people from E2 people. Prior to the disc system Inuit did not think of one another in this numeric form.

The E2 area encompasses an area that is north and west of E1. The E2 area is completely inland as opposed to E1—E1 was a coastal community. Alan points out that those older than himself express that they were "upset by it" meaning the disc system, whereas he is not. Alan's relationship with his disc number would have lasted approximately seven years. He had not been alive when the system was first brought into force, and by the time he was born the system had become common practice and had become normalized just as it was preparing to fade away.

Alan hesitates when I ask if he knew of any Inuit who were angry over the system. After a pause, he chooses the word "upset" to describe how some Inuit felt. Inuit people do not indulge or nurture anger in any form, not even in their language. This behaviour can be considered a form of piiriqatigiingniq, the working together for a common purpose. In this context, it means to not cause rifts between neighbours and community members, or to not give anger a place to grow.

Alan was instructed by his mother to memorize his number and his E-Number remains engraved in his memory. He ends our talk with:

In town here, some people can remember their
disc number okay and talk about it. And all they can

say is that they remember their disc number. Some people remember their disc number and it's just an identification number, and some people have E2 and I don't know about number two (meaning those with E2 discs) but they never talked about it to anyone. Some people got E2 and I don't know how many of them.

What emerged from what remained unsaid in my conversation with Alan is that the disc system had resulted in Inuit seeing each other as somehow different. Inuit would not have associated a region of origin with difference, yet after the introduction of the disc system, they did. In Tikirarjuaq there are two different groups of former disc holders who will tell each other their disc numbers. It becomes a point of reference in terms of geography within a conversation relating to their own inherent sense of ancestral connectivity but at the same time the community members now differentiate from one another based on their E1 or E2 numbers. The disc system brought with it a division in the community that has lasted well beyond the system itself. Alan sums up our time together by saying, "You don't forget that number." These are Alan's most important words.

If the districts and later the distribution of E-necklaces had never occurred, meaning that if the non-Inuit way of cartography and identification had not interfered, the traditional way of understanding each other as Inuit would not have been broken. For Padlei Inuit, we were called "the people of the willow" or "the people from beyond" because we lived inland amongst the small willows in the Keewatin area of northern Manitoba. Some other Inuit groups were called "Ahiarmeun or People of the Berries."[5] To call or name one another based on distance from one another or the landscape that surrounds them contains so much beauty and accuracy. There is no beauty found in being known by a number on a string.

Alan was born eight years prior to the official disbanding of the disc system and his disc number would have, in theory, been active only during his first eight years of life. However, his mother Rosie made a point of showing him his disc and having him memorize his disc number at the time the system was, according to the Canadian government, winding down. Because his involvement with the disc is short-lived this may account for his saying, "It didn't bother me."

Alan's situation shows the wisdom of a mother who had lived through and raised other children within the E-Number system. Rosie Jessie Voisey ensured that her son had memorized his number: It was an act of motherly protection. She was preventing him from any form of future government conflict, an indicator of how the Inuit circumvented government intervention. Alan's experienced mom may not have been aware of or believed in the system being done away with in 1971 and took the precautionary measure of having her young boy commit his number to memory,

---

5   de Coccola, *The Incredible Eskimo*, 181.

explaining only to his elementary school-aged mind that it was, in the words of Alan, "Eskimo Identity." A young boy would not have recognized what the words "Eskimo Identity" meant at that time. What he did recognize is that his mom had asked him to remember something that she considered important. She could find security in knowing her boy had memorized a government-issued number and that he was at least protected from the consequences of not knowing the number. This act of memorization brought her comfort and reassurance where his future safety was concerned. This can be seen as an act of love when forcing a child to remember something that was so important that he can still recall his number without hesitation more than four decades later.

Alan and I end our conversation with laughter. He tells me that it is snowing on the day that we speak and how he had gone into the local store and wished a few people a Merry Christmas, even though it was only mid-September. "One community member wished me Happy New Year." I laugh and say, "Time travels fast in the Arctic!"

My response is based on a sentence my mom used to say to me when I was young. "There's no sweat in the Arctic!" she would say, and we would laugh. It is common for Inuit to bring laughter into hard situations and to never say "good-bye" to one another because Inuit never had greeting words prior to the white man's arrival in the North. Words like "hello" or "how are you" are seen as useless because when we are standing in front of each other we can see how we are. "Goodbye" was not a word brought into use either, simply because there was the understanding that we would see each other again. So instead, Alan and I wish one another good night.

DAVID SERKOAK, OTTAWA, ON
Interview response via email: October 14, 2013

I did not know David Serkoak until a University of Alberta professor brought him to me via an email exchange. I received an email from the professor who was in Labrador and had met David who was there working with Inuit youth. He was at the time a 62-year-old Inuk and cultural educator and continues to do this important work.[6] David is like me, he is Padlei Inuit.

David replied on email the same day. He told me he knew most of the Voiseys in Kivalliq. He mentioned Alan's ataatattiaq (grandfather) Solomon and angaujuk Lewis Voisey. David wrote that he grew up in Tikirarjuaq from 1959–69. "My late late uncle Noah Kaayak was a handy man for Henry Voisey in Padlei Hudson Bay Post in the fifties... Yes, I used to have an E-Number it was E1-602 but lost the disc," he wrote. As with Alan, David began with our connection to one another through our ancestors. There are so few Ahiarmiut or Padlei Inuit left in Canada that it is not only traditional but critical that we make a point of sharing

---

6   Pfeiff, "A Man of Principle," 23–24.

how our blood links us to each other. On August 13, 2013, I emailed David the list of twelve questions along with the consent form and information letter.

The ability to wait is a trait of a good hunter. I was aware that David was travelling throughout the summer. He had said in his email, "I am on the road quite a bit on drum dancing workshops." He is an Inuit Elder who is in demand. I also knew that his access to the internet would be sporadic at best. More importantly though is that I knew that I cannot prod an Elder and that this time of waiting had to be respected. I knew that were I able to be face-to-face in David's home that I would wait for as long as he chose for me to wait between questions, but the circumstances would be the opposite were I interviewing him away from his home. This is an area that non-Inuit researchers need to give thought to. It is simply not appropriate to rush any Elder to answer any question immediately. Despite my own impatience, I knew that I could not send repeated emails or poke at or badger an Elder. I had respect the amount of time that passed, and then I had to spend time with his responses and to understand the wisdom that he extended to my work.[7] Patience is required.

It was not until October 14, two months after our first contact, that I received a reply from David. The wait was long but well worth it. He wrote on the document with the interview questions that he replied on October 11, 2013,

---

7   Oosten & Laugrand, *Interviewing Inuit Elders*, 6-7.

beginning at 6 a.m. and ending at 6:55 a.m. He had given thought to the twelve questions with responses that were brief and to the point. Within each answer were many layers of a life that has been lived with honesty and steadfastness.

David wrote that he "was less than ten years old" when he received his disc and was "not sure when government issued me my Eskimo disc number" but his guess was that it was in the 1950s. He wrote, "In the late fifties after the forced relocations we lived in Arivat (Eskimo Point), Tikirarjuaq (Whale Cove) and Kangiqliniq (Rankin Inlet)." David used the word "forced" and is a survivor of the Ahiarmuit Inuit, who were relocated by the government of Canada several times during the 1950s. Laugrand, Oosten and Serkoak point out in *The Saddest Time of my Life: Relocating the Ahiamiut from Ennadai Lake to Arviat (1950–1958)* that others have written on the forced relocations.[8]

The Ahiamiut were relocated not only from Nueltin and Henik Lakes but also "to Arviat and from Arviat to Tikirarjuaq and Rankin Inlet." David would have, as he states, been less than ten years old when the constant moving began and grew up as a member of an Inuit group who were being flown into and dropped off from one northern community to the next without food, without tools, and without supplies because the government thought that Inuit were able to survive in any environment and were

---

8   Laugrand, Oosten and Serkoak, *The Saddest Time of my Life*, 113–135.

able to make their way without the tools for hunting or basic survival.

While the rest of the world drove cars, went to work in offices, rode around on transit systems, and bought the meat for their tables at various food chains, it was assumed that Inuit Canadians could be dropped in the middle of nowhere and be able to survive. This line of thinking that says Inuit are not modern people and are people who do not work in various professions, and who remain stilled into the time of long ago is one that persists. The government of the 1950s thought nothing of flying Inuit into an unknown place and dropping them off like human waste with the expectation that they could fend for themselves with only the clothes on their backs. This is something that we would not even consider doing to an animal. How can anyone think that it's okay to do this to the Ahiarmiut, the Padlei, the People from Beyond and of the Willow?

David stated in his responses to my questions that the disc number "was for government purposes. I think that they gave us disc numbers for welfare, school, police and medical...I think they cannot pronounce our names because Inuit always used a one-name system traditionally." David wrote that he was "not sure when I lost my disc number, I think it was in the sixties when we were living in Tikirarjuaq and I never got it replaced and I never reported it." He, like many other disc holders, would have memorized his E-Number at a young age.

I find it interesting that David did not report the loss of his physical disc necklace to the authorities. He was able to stop using his disc number "after the government changed our naming system again, this time to surname system like south of 60. My father, my brother and I all have different names," he wrote, "I guess we choose our own Inuit names as surnames." He adds that he never had to make use of the disc number on tax forms or in place of his social insurance number. His reply to how the disc number made him feel is strongly worded, "The Gov't controlled us back then via RCMP, welfare agents and teachers we DO what we were told no questions asked. Back then, my disc number was nothing to me it was used by Qablunaaq only. But, only years later it began to bother me how the Gov't treated us like their (bad) dogs."

David did not go into detail about this emotion of being "treated...like their (bad) dogs." However, his carefully chosen words leave a clear impression of how intrusive the system was for him. David was direct in his statement that he did not feel any sense of attachment toward his number and that it was something that non-Inuit used, not himself. He presented his disc number as something that is separate from his physical self. From our correspondence, it appears that only after he matured did he give any thought to what the disc number represented and it is curious that he chose to bracket the word (bad) in his response, bringing into play the distinction and dichotomy of what a (bad) or (good) dog would represent to non-Inuit.

David is an Inuk who was raised with, maintains, and teaches Inuit traditional ways of life. His response to the next two questions reflects the changing of times. When asked if he ever discussed disc numbers amongst his own community members and why, he responds, "Many Inuit always have regional or by community differences even today by their dialects, community lifestyles etc. not so much by their disc numbers. Racial differences were alive back then just like today among Inuit." David's observation is in opposition to what Alan Voisey had stated when he noted that an Inuit community containing E1 and E2 people, the E2 Inuit showed a difference in attitude toward their disc numbers.

David responded to the last question concerning the greatest impact of the disc system on his community by saying, "It was the beginning of the change in Inuit naming system, not so much to older Inuit back then, today many younger generation has no clue about naming their children traditionally." He noted that "when I got married in early 1970s, my official papers were still mixed up, so I hired a lawyer to change everything to Serkoak."

David's experience is a summation of a life riddled with colonial disorder and demonstrates the use of a colonial construct. It points to the constant government interference that David had lived with from infancy to well into his twenties. David's life was a life of uncertainty. When he was small the RCMP bust up a drum dance in his parents' tent and he and his family were victims of repeated relocations of the Padlei. When David finally tired of government intervention in his life, he hired a lawyer and had all his legal documents changed over to Serkoak. Making use of a lawyer was the one thing David could do to stop the government from making any further changes in his life. He legalized his last name to prevent further government invasiveness. The law is a language government officials understand, and David learned to use it to his advantage. His youth years were spent with the government flying him and his family members from one community to the next, often leaving them without food or the tools required to maintain or sustain life in their new place of abode. Later he became a numbered Inuk and recalls Project Surname: "I remember Abe Okpik came to Tikirarjuaq in the sixties visiting every household recording new name system."

Although David's early life was one of constant motion and change, he continues to do the one thing that has kept him alive and well through all the upheaval—he adheres to and lives his life according to Inuit traditional knowledge. He has devoted his life to keeping and spreading this knowledge to others through drum dancing workshops and education. It is work that encompasses the spirit of Inuit life, the isuma of it all. In this way, David Serkoak upholds and nourishes not only himself but with all he comes into contact. David Serkoak is a survivor in the truest sense of the word.

What was fun for me is that I ran into David at the Edmonton International Airport a few months after our email exchange. We were both heading to the washroom.

We knocked shoulders and I said, "Zebedee?" and he said, "No. David." I introduced myself and we laughed over meeting each other this way. I had my son take a picture of us together. I thanked him for the generous comments that he supplied. He thanked me for writing of him so well.

Inuit are beautiful to one another.

MARTHA HATKAITOK,
AT MARTHA'S HOME IN EDMONTON, AB
Date: January 8, 2014, 1:45 p.m.

I met Martha in the spring of 2013 while fulfilling hours with a community service learning project I was part of through the University of Alberta. She was working as the receptionist at the Edmonton Inuit Cultural Society and the first day we talked with one another her hair was long and in a single braid down her back. She had on old blue sweatpants and a heavy sweater. She was beading what would become a doll and her work was beautiful and careful. We talked about who we each are and who our relatives are. She knew of my Voisey cousins in Tikirarjuaq. Martha had a quiet, happy voice and the best smile.

She told me her disc story that day, but as I needed the information for my research, I knew I needed ethics approval from the university before I could use any information she gave me. I applied as soon as I could and received approval in July 2013. I tried finding Martha again, but EICS was closed. I sent an email to their president. No response. I went down to EICS a couple of times, but the door was always locked. One day I spoke with a lady who worked at the nearby Canadian Native Friendship Centre. She told me that all the furniture from EICS had been removed. I emailed the president again and again got no response. My hunt for Martha became a full-time pursuit.

I was able to find an EICS board member through social media. I was worried that this contact would think I only had ulterior motives when I became her friend, I waited sixty days before I asked her about Martha. I think of it as another form of waiting during the hunt.

She replied that she and Martha had parted ways the week prior to Christmas 2013 and hadn't exchanged phone numbers. Early in January 2014, I again sent an email to the president of the EICS. It was met with the by now expected silence. Then, on the night of January 7, Martha called, saying the EICS president had told her she better call me. I was thrilled. I arranged an interview for the following afternoon.

Before I left my house, I put on my oldest sweatpants, an old sweater, and the winter jacket that I kept promising myself I would throw out but never did. I didn't want to look like the snobby, university Inuk. I wanted to look like everyone else. When I arrived at Martha's house, she was wearing a nice dress, with a beaded necklace and had recently cut and styled her hair to a short braid-less, more current, fashion. A dab of makeup lay on her beautiful northern face. I felt like a slob next to her. "She dressed for me," I thought and smiled inside myself.

In our conversation, Martha noted how she finds the adjustment to city life a daily task. She had moved to Edmonton from Baker Lake, NU, three years prior. She looked healthy, bright, and happy to have company. She was full of fun and we laughed easily together. She was sewing a parka the day I am there. She had gifted hands, clever hands, and I felt comfortable with her. Martha was open and honest in her views on the disc system, and I remain grateful for her and what she told me.

As we sat there talking, Martha pauses as she tells me that she was either one or two years old when she received her disc. As her memories return, the pace of her words accelerates. "I'm pretty sure I was two years old because that was the time when I got picked up out on the land and they took me to Baker Lake, and then to ah, Churchill, MB... for tuberculosis."

In one short sentence Martha had noted the consequences of two government policies in the North. The first being the issuing of a disc number and the second being removed from the land, her home. She is sent away because of the tuberculosis epidemic. Government policy during the tuberculosis outbreaks in the mid-twentieth century was to place Inuit in medical facilities across Canada. Sick Inuit were transported by boat, which made it difficult to return during the short thaw. That simple geographical fact is coupled with the fact that Inuit did not receive a ticket to return home, and many could not and did not return They stayed away for an average of two and a half years while they received treatment, and during this time, many families did not know where their loved ones had been sent or received updates on their condition. The result has been that many Inuit still mistrust the health care system, and many remember the trauma of having a loved one taken away for x-rays, and never returning, or not having their bodies returned for burial.

Because of her age, I ask Martha how long she lived on the land. She tells me that it was not until 1969, when she was twelve, that she and her family moved into a house. "We lived in igloos and tents." I remarked that there are few people alive today who can attest to this traditional form of housing. Martha replies without hesitation, "The only problem was...we didn't know we had to pay for the house every month," and she adds in a voice that comes out as a soft song, "We were used to being rent-free tenants with rent-free kitchens!" We both laugh at the way she has expressed this foreign concept of once being a free moving, non-monetary group to becoming a sedentary family with rent to pay. Dissolving traditional ways of life and forcing Inuit into regulated settlements is yet another way in which the state tried to enforce its sovereignty over the North.

Martha tells me that she received her disc necklace in Baker Lake and her earliest memory of using her disc number was when the census people came to town. "They asked about our E2 numbers and not our names..." and says she doesn't recall using the "E-Number in school but I do remember using it for when they were putting us in hostels for residential school."

And just like that our conversation turns from the account of a small girl's experience with census takers and the use of her E-Number instead of her name to the matter-of-fact use of that same number for residential school purposes. I am jolted by how Martha talks about the impact of government intervention in a matter-of-fact way, and not as something to be pitied.

Not only did Martha receive her disc in Baker Lake but she also attended residential school there. Our conversation turns briefly to residential school. Martha tells me how she would be "flown into Back River or wherever my parents were but there was a certain spot that my parents had to meet the plane to pick us up" for summer break. "Just when school was over, we were sent home, but I remember the pilot asking for our E-tag numbers...every time we boarded the plane."

There is something unsettling about how Martha speaks about her childhood as though going from living on the land to being tagged with an E-Number and later being confined to residential school and living in a hostel is normal. She does not display any form of emotion as she speaks. The disc system and residential schools as simply considered "normal."

Martha tells me that she did not wear her disc number regularly. "No, I memorized mine," and she melodically sings her number out as though it is a jingle for an advertisement. She says, "My parents kept it all the time because they were afraid we might lose it. Sometimes I would have it around my neck, but I didn't like it." Martha goes on to say that her mother had replaced the government-issued string on the necklace with "braided caribou sinew."

Martha's mom had taken the time to remove the original string and replace it with not only something that she saw as stronger and more secure but with something that would also represent an Inuit component of daily living— caribou sinew. The braiding together of caribou sinew can be interpreted as both a form of compliance and as resistance to a government policy.

Martha had her disc with her until she moved to Gjoa Haven, when someone threw it away. She did seek a replacement. "I called down to Indian and Northern Affairs but they said they don't have those anymore...I remember trying to call them in '79."

By 1979 when she called, the disc system was being dissolved but Martha seemed unaware of that. Having that necklace had become so commonplace in her life that she assumed it was an item that should always be with her, like a driver's licence. I ask Martha whether she felt bitter about her experiences. Her response says much about the Inuit view of the world: "No, we don't hold a grudge that long." Inuit do not express anger outwardly or harbour it inwardly. Despite the things she has had to endure, Martha still remembers her traditional upbringing.

Martha returns to her first encounter with a census taker,

> I remember the person who was doing the census. Because my parents were out on the land, he asked me for my age. I said, "I don't know." I was so young and he just guessed my age...there was a bunch of us from Back River, our ages were guessed. Like my cousins.

Inuit did not record birth dates and years on a calendar the way Westerners do. Like my own anaana, Martha is a paperless Inuk. She could be much younger than age fifty-seven.

Martha indicates that she doesn't know if her disc number was ever used in place of her social insurance number but answers that her disc

> made me feel uncomfortable. I'm a person with a name. I'm not a person with a number. Like a military person or RCMP officer. It made me feel, what the heck! I'm not from the military! After coming back from, after tuberculosis, I found this to be very strange. People using E-numbers instead of their names.

Martha spent four years in a TB asylum and returned home to discover that E-Number usage had become common practice. She would have been approximately six years old.

Martha then recounts the story of the RCMP officer who had taken her away to Churchill on her journey to the TB sanatorium and how this officer returned to look for her years later, but she wasn't home at the time. "I walked into my granny's house and she goes, 'There was a police officer here from way back and he was looking for you.'" Her grandmother offered no further details and Martha didn't ask, "because we don't talk to our Elders like that."

It took Martha a few years to discover who the police officer was because she adhered to the traditional practice of never asking an Elder a question and waiting for an Elder to disclose information of their own accord. She had to wait for her grandmother to reveal that information. She is still touched by the officer's interest in her well-being. This story shows that some enforcers of the disc system did show compassion and interest in the people that they had to work with. It could also be Martha's way of showing how she does not bear a grudge herself.

Martha says the disc number made her think of herself and other Inuit differently.

> It felt so wrong to be called, "Hey, E2...!" And there
> was one time when I said, "Hey you know," I was just
> a kid and I said, "Hey I got a name too—like you!"...

I got in trouble for that, I remember that, saying to some person doing the Saturday grocery thing for the hostel...they wanted to know how many kids were in the hostel and what number each one had.

In a real sense E-numbers had become a form of financial budgeting for the residential school Martha attended and a form of financial accountability by those who ran the school to the government of Canada and the local store.

The residual effect of the disc system among survivors is complex. Martha expresses both gratitude and remorse. "I mean, the government helped us with food and stuff like that and we really appreciated that and our family allowance, stuff like that. The E-numbers were...I didn't like that very much. It felt like the government owned us and ran our lives."

There is a sense of loss of the ownership of one's own life, something that Martha did not like. Martha feels that "back then we were afraid of the white people. We did everything they asked us to do. We agreed to everything." She closes with a laugh and says, "I want the world to know about this mess!"

Martha is a strong Inuk woman who has lived a life of constant change. She is sincere and frank in her responses to the questions in our talk. It was an experience of honour for me to sit in her kitchen, to laugh with her and to hear the words of an Inuk woman who survived not only the disc system but also residential school and life inside a tuberculosis sanatorium. Her early life was laden with experiences of government policy and intervention, but she continues to hold onto her own Inuk spirit of happiness and tradition.

When she comments on "wanting everyone to know about this mess," I have to wonder if her words refer only to the disc system, or whether she is referring to the constant intrusion of various types of colonial bureaucratic control throughout her early life.

Martha asked me for only one thing—to not have her disc number placed anywhere near her name in the writing of her story. I have honoured that request.

ZEBEDEE NUNGAK,
204 URIUQ KANGIRSUK, QC
Date: February 7, 2014

I took a chance and looked up Zebedee Nungak's phone number online. I was surprised it was sitting there in front of me on my screen. I could not find a contact email for him even though I had emailed other Inuk people I knew of who worked with him through the Avataq Cultural Institute and had contacted them in my hunt for Mr. Nungak.

On January 29, 2014, I looked him up on Canada 411. It was important to me to interview the author of "E9-1956," published in 2000, one of the few publications by an Inuk writer on the Eskimo Identification Canada system. Zebedee Nungak is a cultural leader, spokesperson, politician, writer, and inspiration to many Inuit Canadians. He is what is known as an "Experimental Eskimo"—one of several Inuit children who were removed from their home communities and placed into southern Canadian cities as requested by the government of Canada in the early 1960s.[9]

The purpose of this experiment was to prove whether Inuit children had the ability to learn beyond Grades Five or Six. Mr. Nungak, along with Peter Ittinaur and Eric Tagoona, filed a lawsuit against the Canadian government in 2008 for this experiment and have yet to receive any form of compensation. The Harper government had indicated that payment had been made to residential school survivors and that it would not extend further compensation to survivors of the Experimental Eskimo project. Jody Wilson-Raybould, minister of justice and attorney general of Canada, met with the trio when she was with the Liberal cabinet between 2015 and 2021. Their case remains in the court system.

Despite some of his life experiences, Zebedee is known for his humour. Among all the many occupations he has had he continues to focus on promoting the use of the Inuktitut language and Inuit education. Zebedee is a highly respected Elder and because of all his successes, I was terrified to speak to him.

I need not have worried. Zebedee is fun. He made me laugh about ten times in our first two minutes of

9 Greenwald, Barry, dir. *Experimental Eskimos*. Toronto, ON: White Pine Pictures and Paunna Productions, 2009.

conversation. I briefly explained who I am and asked if I could email him the interview questions prior to recording our phone interview. He kindly agreed and gave me his personal email address, while cautioning me that the disc system is not something he views with anger. I sent Zebedee the questions right away and in his response, he granted me an interview on February 7, 2014.

When I called on the appointed day, I again felt nervous to speak to someone who has devoted his life to the future generations of Inuit. I respect this man whose hand I've never shaken. He is a true leader.

Zebedee answered my first two questions together, telling me, "By the time I was baptized on January 2, 1952, I must have been given (the disc number). The RCMP had passed through our camp and my baptism certificate which is issued on January 2 has me down as E9-1956." The E9 district represents the northern coastal area of Quebec, now named Nunavik. Zebedee is the first Inuk I had spoken to who gave me any indication that his disc number was used on other identification documents, and this revelation shows a relationship between church and state on paper.

Because Zebedee had made use of the word "camp" in his response, I ask him if he and his family were living out on the land at the time of his birth. He says, "We were living at a certain location. In today's language it would be a camp because it's not an established full-time community, but the place where I was born is called Sapuutiligait." Not knowing the exact day that the RCMP issued his disc necklace,

Zebedee says he would have been about eight months old based on his birth certificate. Since I wanted to know how the disc number operated around day-to-day living, I asked Zebedee how he made use of his disc number. This included attending school or visiting a doctor. Zebedee chided me when he replied:

> There's no such thing as visiting a doctor...and there's no such thing as school until 1959 but by that time we were using our names and not just numbers. But in the place of visiting a doctor, I was sent to hospital for treatment of early-stage tuberculosis in 1956 and that's when my actual disc was lost. I had it around my neck. We used to wear them around our necks all the time if we had reason to but I lost my number when I went to hospital in Moose Factory.

Zebedee would have been four years old when he lost the disc necklace at the time of his departure to Moose Factory, and yet even at that age he had his number memorized. He reminds me how important disc numbers were:

> Because Eskimo disc numbers were the only thing that were of identity purposes everyone knew their number so I've never forgotten that I was E9-1956 even though the thing was lost in 1956—that's how deeply ingrained it was.

Knowing his number, in this instance, made his identity clear to the people around him and served a practical purpose. When I ask Zebedee if he ever sought out a replacement he replies matter-of-factly:

In 1956 there was no federal office. Federal information was very sketchy to say the least and it was just the RCMP patrolling by boat or by dog team in the winter. I don't think they had a lot of spare discs on hand to replace the ones that were lost.

When I asked if his disc number was used on the filing of income tax, Zebedee says, "No. By the time we started paying taxes our names were in use. When I say our names were in use, my name, Zebedee Nungak, is actually my given name and not my family name." Zebedee indicates that he left home in 1963 prior to the standardization of his family's surname. His family members had adopted his grandfather's name "Tulugak" in 1967. He was not a part of this change and in his words, "I've always carried my given name." Zebedee explains that the adoption of surnames began in his community in the mid-1960s and "before that we were just hunters and fisherman and trappers."

I ask Zebedee what he thought of the disc. His response is stoical:

Back when I was growing up we didn't have a lot of people complaining that it looked like a dog tag or a prisoner's number or talk. It was just a simple fact of life that all Eskimos had disc numbers and the government issued them. They (meaning Inuit) didn't have any hand in assigning them or designing them. It was strictly a federal practice to identify Inuit by that system but I don't recall anyone complaining about how these were used.

Zebedee makes a point of not speaking of self in this instance. He instead thinks about his own community members and the fact that no one criticized the use of the system. He approaches the disc as a fact of life, a way of communicating to others. However, he does make a point of saying that the Inuit had no input into the disc system:

> I rather lament that they discontinued (the disc). The government simply let it piffle out without justifying why they did it in the first place and I'm still trying to track down a novelty store that can do an exact replica of my disc number. I'll get one of my children's disc numbers, like the actual thing, just have them do the crown on the one side and the number on the other side and I'd have it embossed in a gold frame or wear it around my neck with a gold chain.

He laughs and has low giggles coming from his throat as he says this. Zebedee treats the possible resurrection of his number with humour and a certain amount of glee. He describes the revival of his disc as an event to be shared with his children, as if a party should be happening at the same time and a disc should be hung in gold frame as a centre piece memorial. There is a lovely irony at the thought of it all, but Zebedee through all this humour, does raise an important point—the government never formally announced the dissolution of a system that they never formally announced they were instituting.

Unlike many other Inuit, Zebedee has taken control of the story of his disc, turning it into a positive:

> I know that some Inuit will make a big speech about it, about how it looks like a dog tag and a prisoner's number and that people shouldn't have to be identified this way but I look at it as a uniquely Inuit thing, a very Eskimo thing, only the Eskimos were ever issued this, and I thought that was quite a status to have...it's a government invention but it's unique to Inuit and that's how I see it.

It's a different way of thinking about the disc, and about other forms of identification the government issues. In the words of Zebedee:

> I rather lament all these others, the social insurance number and the health number and beneficiary numbers and all these other piles of modern identification that are issued nowadays and overwhelm

the disc number. I still have an admiration for it. I still think the government owes an explanation as to why they established it and ask us if we agree to having it discontinued.

What troubles Zebedee is not that this system existed, but the fact that Inuit were never called together and told why the disc system was coming to life. All many Inuit knew was that they had to have the disc with them at all times and had to have their number memorized. He concludes by noting that the federal government did not ask if Inuit wanted the system to be dismantled. I think this a reflection on a colonial system that never had permission from Inuit to start or stop the system even though the Inuit are those most affected by it.

Zebedee ends our interview on the Eskimo Identification Canada system by saying, "It became an administrative convenience for those who were administering these things." The practicality of the system through the use of one instead of several numbers as well as a disc being a unique form of Inuit identity is how Zebedee views the entire system. Yet there is that one lingering issue—not having a government celebration or explanation to its installation or disappearance.

Zebedee is a wonderful Inuk man to speak with, to laugh with and to whom I am grateful. His perspective makes us think about why the government never created a celebration or provided an explanation directly to Inuit and instead hides behind three documents with ever-shrinking information in each. Why hasn't there been an official apology of the system? Why, even to this day, do Inuit not have a full understanding of a system that became a part of their daily lives?

CHAPTER EIGHT

isummaniq

(Can think, understand, has reached the age of reasoning)

I have spoken on the Eskimo Identification Canada system at many conferences across Canada. On my home campus at the University of Alberta, in Edmonton, I teach the Eskimo Identification Canada system in every class that I instruct regardless of the course. At the end of each presentation or class, there are always common responses. I am amazed at the responses from the audience, but try to understand how audience members have arrived at their understandings of what I had presented. I consider how to fill in those gaps in their knowledge, and mine. I have reshaped the presentation over and over again. The following addresses the common responses from the many audiences who gave of their time and interest in the Eskimo Identification Canada system.

ESKIMO IDENTIFICATION CANADA SYSTEM NUMBER
VERSUS SOCIAL INSURANCE NUMBER

What I have found most often is that non-Inuit equate the Eskimo Identification Canada system to their own social insurance number or a driver's licence number and speak as though there is no reason to be upset with the system. It is common for the dominant members of any one society to look upon the marginalized and choose not to recognize assimilation or colonization or the continued impacts of forced government policy as something to be upset over simply because it does not affect them in any direct way. After all, Indigenous Canadians are only good at one thing and that is their continued complaining and wanting to be paid out for policies from long ago.

When I hear that response, the response of, "It's only a number and we all have a social insurance number," I think about how my audience managed to miss the most important point of what had just been presented to them. Without a disc number, Inuit Canadians were denied access to the same benefits that all other Canadians used daily. If you didn't have your disc or had not memorized that number or were unable to provide that number, you did not have access to needed medical attention while all other Canadian citizens freely went to a doctor without having memorized a number. Without a disc number, you were not able to buy goods or trade furs. No disc number meant you could not engage in any economic activity; in other words, no disc number meant no food, no supplies, no sugar, no flour, no tobacco. Non-Inuit were not barred from any form of foods or other items. Without a disc number your children were not allowed to sit in a classroom because a disc number is what granted your children entrance to education, the same education that all other Canadian children received without a disc number. Without a disc number Inuit grandparents were not able to access benefits granted to all other elderly Canadians who did not have a disc number.

What audiences sometimes do not grasp is that Inuit names carry the importance of all of our ancestors. Inuit names and ancestral characteristics transcend generation after generation as do the characteristics of those who went ahead of us. Our beginnings and our endings lie in the names of our ancestors. Our names are a remembrance of our Elders, those who broke trail before and for us. Our names carry their love and their tenacity. Our names remind us of the goodness of those who made it possible for our new generations to be here.

I am often questioned on my own authenticity. It is a way that people measure me. When I hear Inuit youth say that they have no traditional understandings or training, I invite them to speak to the Elders of their communities and if there are no Inuit Elders available, I say speak to a First Nation or Métis Elder. Reach out and discover what lies within your blood. Inuit ways of knowing and being do not disappear because time marches past us. Inuit blood contains Inuit memory. Seek it out and believe in it. Ask why you were given the name that you were given.

I am named after a sister to my father who died in childhood. My mother followed through on the tradition of naming that she held to be true. She consulted with the one woman who would have been her Elder at the time, my father's mom, and it was from her that my name received clearance. This same pattern of naming occurred with the arrival of my sons and this same tradition has been granted to my grandchildren whereby they carry the names of their Elders, my parents and myself. Non-Inuit may argue that I do not have an Inuit name, but that is not the point. The real point is that the Inuit traditional naming processes have been carried through, first by my mom then myself and now my own sons.

To the Inuit youth in our world right now, go find yourself by finding your Elders, parents and aunties and uncles. Your name holds as much importance as you do. Take it back and own it and when some non-Inuit person says that a social insurance number holds the same importance as a disc number, get them to read this book.

EICS VERSUS THE PASS SYSTEM

Often assimilative practices, policies and forms of state harm that were directed and laid upon First Nations Canadians are placed onto Inuit Canadians with a view of pan-Indigeneity. I don't even want to know how many times I have said, "I am not an Indian," and I say that though assimilation, colonialism, imperialism, and other forms of social power follow a distinct pattern with the end result being the same—complete control. However, Inuit are not included under the provisions of the Indian Act and therefore Inuit did not operate under the unofficial pass system that was administered by Indian agents on First Nation reserves across Canada.

The pass system limited the mobility of First Nations people, meaning it also limited their access to commerce, creating their own industry and the simple act of shopping. The pass system limited the freedom of movement that all other Canadians not living on a reserve enjoyed.

The disc number did not limit the mobility of Inuit Canadians in the sense of movement, but it did place a heavy form of surveillance on Inuit families in that the disc number recorded where Inuit lived and traded, along with where they hunted and where they traded their furs for market. The disc number was in effect an early GPS system that told not only government officials but also Hudson's Bay Company management who traded what fur on what date, where and for how much. It also detailed the annual income of an Inuk trapper and his family and then moved on to tracking what goods were purchased at a trading post. The lives of Inuit Canadians were a transparent record of personal information that could be made available to Canadian government officials and to those who marketed and sold the furs in Europe.

Inuit did not live on reserves, but through forced relocation were moved into small northern communities all for the sake of making Canadian state sovereignty visible in the North.

If there ever was a limitation to mobility it lies in the government's ill-planned and ill-executed system of relocation and their need to populate northern shorelines post-World War II. Once Inuit were removed from the land and brought into small hamlets, their freedom of movement was later limited by the killing of dog teams and the introduction of schools and town life. I will never say the old ways disappeared, but new methods of hunting were introduced through snowmobiles and guns—the same items used by hunters in the south. The essence of tradition does not change but methods can.

Trying to correlate the disc system to the pass system is at best an under-informed comparison.

EICS VERSUS HOLOCAUST SURVIVORS' TATTOOS

The numbering of humanity was not a new idea by the time the government of Canada placed the Eskimo Identification Canada system into full practice. I bring up the tattooing of survivors of the Holocaust as this numbering system has been brought to my attention when I've spoken about the disc system. The Holocaust was horrific and the amount of death that was brought upon the Jewish population is not comparable in terms of tragedy. How do we measure horror?

When World War II finally ended, those who managed to survive concentration camps left with a permanent reminder of their experience based on a number tattooed into their wrist. In all of this destruction of humanity, I do have to say that once the survivors arrived back home, if they did at all, the number on their wrist and all the inhumane treatment they had experienced did not limit their access to the benefits extended to them by their governments. That number never came into play again in terms of surveillance and support.

Making this comparison, one that audiences have directed to me, places me in an an uncomfortable position. I often wonder about the audience members who bring this comparison forward and how their minds work in the area of inhumanity and how the slaughter of millions of humans can equate to a disc number. The disc number was not created as a form of recording the genocide of an entire ethnicity.

EICS VERSUS THE NUMBERING SYSTEM OF INDIAN RESIDENTIAL SCHOOLS

The Indian Residential School system ran in Canada officially from 1883–1996 and was a force-filled form of assimilation for all Inuit, First Nations, and Métis children. My mother served eight years at a school just outside of Winnipeg and was taken from her family when she was approximately seven years old. She was released when she was sixteen as that was the expected age of release. (The age for release from a residential school later became eighteen years.)

When I present on the Eskimo Identification Canada system, I am often reminded that First Nations children also had their names removed, were issued biblical Christian names and a number. During the course of their stay, First Nations, Métis and Inuit children had their numbers written onto their clothing and were called out in school by their numbers and not their names.[1] What is more confusing with the residential school numbering system is that the number often changed during the course of the child's time served, meaning that the child may have been placed into a position of having to memorize a new number every year.

Numbers are an attempt to remove the human element, but they can not remove the human being. The residential school numbering system is a cold representation of a First Nations child forced into a system of brutal assimilation and for myself as the child of an eight full-year survivor of residential school, I know what the first generation of children of survivors can experience.

I would never diminish the experience of all First Nations and Métis children who share with Inuit the experience of how a number attempts to dehumanize. Being called out by a number instead of your traditional name, the name your parents gave you before you saw the sky and bestowed upon you at birth, and having that name

---

1   Douglas Quan, "'Assault' on Residential School Students' Identities Began the Moment they Stepped Inside," *National Post.* June 2, 2015. https://nationalpost.com/news/canada /assault-on-residential-school-students-identities-began-the -moment-they-stepped-inside.

replaced by a European name and later a number, is only one example of what must have been a bewildering childhood experience.

The residential school system operated on shame to create conformity. If we shame a child by eliminating their name and replacing it with a number, how much greater is the experience of belittlement, subservience and ultimately adherence to the demands of non-Indigenous authoritarians? And how much guilt was removed from the colonizer who called out a number instead of a name to address a child? The numbering of First Nations and Métis children reduced or eliminated the sense of compassion and caring that non-Indigenous authoritarians carried and, in many ways, resulted in those in charge conforming to the ultimate goal of assimilation. If the human instinct of compassion is removed, the colonizer will fall in line.

ESKIMO IDENTIFICATION CANADA SYSTEM IN INUIT DAY SCHOOLS

The Inuit residential school experience occurs much later in comparison to First Nations and Métis Canadians. While the residential school system was shutting down south of sixty, it was opening up north of sixty. By 1948 in the south Indian residential schools were preparing to close, while in 1955 in Canada's North the residential school model had only just begun.[2] Inuit children were moved into hostels, the equivalent of residential school dormitories.

The 1960s saw schools being brought into the North with the expectation that an Inuk child would walk into an isolated building, resulting in the separation of children from their families. Inuit families arrived from winter and summer camps, bringing their children into established communities to attend school. The separation of the child from the parents is inconceivable to Inuit. The parents were always the people responsible to teach their child how to survive on the tundra and how to be a good person. In order to keep the family together, the family set up encampments around the schools. The RCMP considered it loitering and bothersome.

A 1961 RCMP report from Clyde River states:

[If] the camp Eskimo children started to attend school regularly there could be some trouble with loitering. The main reason for the loitering would be the parents being reluctant to leave their children in school, as this would tend to "break up" the family as the Eskimos refer to the situation. It is felt that most of the trouble would come from the Eskimo mother.[3]

---

2   Milloy, *A National Crime*, 190.

3   QIA, *Qimmiliriniq*, 20.

What we can understand from the police report is that the colonizer understood the importance of not only an Inuit family but also the importance of the Inuit child. Inuit children, like all other Indigenous Canadian children, were expected to learn the skills required for life at home with their parents and siblings. What we are also seeing is the innovative way that Inuit families followed through with the school requirement. Their children were brought into the community and walked into a school alone while their families camped outside the building waiting for them to complete their school day. It is ridiculous that the RCMP considered this situation problematic and considered charging families with loitering while pointing out that the Inuit mother would be the most reluctant to give her child over to a school system and the most problematic person in the situation.

Inuit were never invited or negotiated into the numbered treaties that exist along the Canadian prairies and the word "Inuit" remains undefined by the federal government. What I take from those two facts is how the federal government has always demonstrated an unwillingness to deal directly with Inuit until the Inuit began to demand land claims negotiations. Inuit Canadians continue to be treated as an afterthought.

The government transferred their understandings of Indian residential schools to the North instead of creating an Inuit-based educational system for Inuit children. In other words, the government stuck with the methods of education created through Indian residential schools and instilled that form of education and learning into the North. The irony remains that children in Nunavut continue to be taught the Alberta curriculum in 2022 and have an attrition rate that holds around 60 per cent. School remains a place of disconnect, especially after forced relocation of Inuit into settlements.

What is different is that when Inuit children arrived at residential school, they arrived already numbered through the Eskimo Identification Canada system. Many would have already memorized the number that would have followed them into adulthood, into marriage, into the birthing of their own children, who would be numbered at birth themselves and very likely the system would transfer onto their grandchildren and ultimately their great grandchildren. Their number would stay with them long after their time was served in a residential school.

This is the point: the Eskimo Identification Canada system number was a life-long symbol.

It was the symbol that replaced your name.
It was the symbol that government officials
   recognized you by.
It was the symbol that supplied you with the basic
   needs of human life.
It was the symbol that allowed you access to human
   rights.

> The E-Number never disappeared once you finished
>   school.
> The E-Number never stained your wrist, it dangled
>   from your neck.
> The E-Number never forced you to stay in one place,
>   but it told others where you were.
> The E-Number never allowed tax exemptions; Inuit
>   pay all tax and carry SIN cards.

The E-Number symbolized all that was wrong with the successive Canadian governments that sustained its use for more than thirty years. The E-Number symbolized the blatant dehumanizing of the smallest Indigenous population in Canada. The E-Number system remains a system that not one government to date has acknowledged or taken responsibility for. Inuit are still waiting for an apology for the disc system.

In keeping the system silenced and not spoken of broadly by any prime minister, Inuit continue to be unacknowledged casualties of colonization, through the deep-rooted breakage of the Inuit naming system that maintained the essence of Inuit life and the ceremony associated with death.

Canadians have witnessed several apologies by our governments. The historic 2008 apology for the Indian Residential School issued by the Harper government was seen as a positive step on the road to reconciliation. Yet Inuit wait to hear an apology for the Eskimo Identification Canada system. I have sat face-to-face with some Inuit who speak as though the number system was not something that bothered them. I have had them tell me in person how they have an affection for their number and that it is a part of who they feel they are.

For me, as someone who never had a disc number or had to manage my life with one, when I hear that kind of talk, I think of how that is all it takes. All it ever takes for any government or corporation to walk away from their responsibility for any harm they may have extended to Inuit Canadians is to have that one Inuk say, "It didn't bother me," and that is what they run with. That is how colonial exoneration is achieved. That is how the Inuit who did feel harm or shame or dehumanization are again ignored and not recognized.

I can not speak for everyone, but I can trouble other people's thinking. I can make others give thought to what appears to be a simple harmless system that did not create physical death but did try to extinguish a traditional system of naming. I can make others give thought to how long-lasting and ignored systems of government can remain in place for decade-upon-decade and how normalization seeps into the consciousness of both the casualties and creators of a system and how it becomes acceptable. It became normal to the point that in time having an E-Number is an expected part of daily existence and those Inuit who were without a number became the outcasts.

When I made application for Nunavut beneficiary status in 2001 and was unable to provide a disc number and could not provide a disc number from my mother, I was left with no immediate government proof of my own Inuit blood and that is wrong. To have my own Inuitness questioned based on a system that had long since closed down prior to my application is an example of the lasting echoes of the Eskimo Identification Canada system.

Before sending the documents through the fax machine I had to supply long form birth certificates on myself and my sons. I was born in Quebec and getting the long form birth certificate from that province took a very long time. I knew that all of our paperwork would have been forwarded into Tikirarjuaq (Place Where Many Gather) or Whale Cove, Nunavut. What had started out as a watching a few months fall off the calendar became a couple of years. Becoming an accepted member of the Nunavut Land Claims Agreement was a long but worthwhile wait.

Inuit membership is based on having ancestral ties to a community. Our applications would have been read through and talked about by the Elders and community members of Tikiratjuaq. There is no federal government input or intervention in the process. Membership into a land claims agreement is controlled solely by the Inuit themselves. It was a glorious day when all of our membership cards arrived in the mailbox. It was a warm sense of being valued and belonging to my own. The Inuit.

Along with this sense of belonging came a different kind of unease—knowing that the legacy of the disc system lives on in my own life. My sons' growing up years were spent in

Edmonton Housing, the name of the city's subsidized housing. When my boys and I came to Edmonton, it was the place that social services moved us into. I had thought I could work our way out of there within four years, but it took twice as long. The first two years in Edmonton we were a welfare family. I worked so very hard at keeping the townhouse that we were in as clean as clean could be. I worked hard at washing and ironing all my sons' clothes. I did not want them to look like they were on welfare, even though our address told their schools that we were.

The lingering sense of unease was the slow realization that I was like my mom, in that I never let my children identify as Inuit while they were in school. We were Edmonton Housing people, and there would be no additional layering of what they were according to a school system. They would not be segregated. They would not be coded as Indigenous students. We were already in the cycle of poverty, but we didn't have to look it or allow anyone to classify us further. I began cleaning at night, and during the day for various companies and families. They paid in cash. The social workers never had to know about that income. Eventually I landed a job in a warehouse, and in time I began working in their office. My sons and I finally moved out of Edmonton Housing. I began to learn how to transport freight around the world. I spent the next seventeen years as a logistician with three different globally based companies.

When my sons graduated from high school, I told them that they must now begin to identify as Inuit. It was hard for them, because they carry their father's French last name. They followed through though, and it wasn't until they each left home that I allowed them to carry their Nunavut beneficiary cards in their wallets. Their beneficiary cards became their parting gift from me in the same sense my own beneficiary card had been the parting gift from my Inuk mom.

The knowledge that the legacy of the disc system lingers in these quiet ways is perhaps the ultimate indication of how deeply the government's policies continue to affect Inuit.

For all the Inuit that I have met and with whom I've spoken and who did feel less than human, for all the Inuit who have asked me why they had a number and why they are now without one, for all the Inuit who have survived a form of damage that can not be seen outwardly, I will not say I am sorry.

I will say that like always you have made it through.

We made it through because Inuit have always been more than a number.

Bibliography

Aglukark, Susan. "E186." *Unsung Heroes.* 1999. YouTube Video. Posted April 2, 2009. https://www.youtube.com/watch?v=BtbZsRYASjU.

Alia, Valerie. *Names & Nunavut Culture and Identity in the Inuit Homeland.* New York: Berghahn Books, 2007.

Angulalik, Jana. "Behind the Inuit Tattoo Revival: Once Banned, Now the Ancient Markings Are Making a Comeback." *Atlantic News,* April 5, 2021. https://www.saltwire.com/atlantic-canada/news/behind-the-inuit-tattoo-revival-once-banned-now-the-ancient-markings-are-making-a-comeback-100574002/.

Arnaquq, Naullaq. "Uqaujjuusiat: Gifts of Words of Advice: Schooling, Education, and Leadership in Baffin Island." In *Sivumut: Towards the Future together, Inuit Women Educational Leaders in Nunavut and Nunavik,* edited by Fiona Walton and Darlene O'Leary, 13–14. Toronto: Women's Press, 2015.

Aupilaarjuk, Mariano et al. "Pisiit, Songs." In *Interviewing Inuit Elders: Perspectives on Traditional Law,* vol. 2, edited by Frederic Laugrand, Jarich Oosten and Wim Rasing, 201–19. Iqaluit: Nunavut Arctic College, 1999.

Backhouse, Constance. *Colour-Coded: A Legal History of Racism in Canada 1900–1950.* Toronto: University of Toronto Press, 1999.

Birket-Smith, Kaj. *Caribou Eskimos: Material and Social Life and their Cultural Position.* Oslo: Gyldendalske Boghandel, 1924.

Bonesteel, Sarah. "The E-Number Identification System." In *Canada's Relationship with the Inuit: A History of Policy and Program,* edited by Erik Anderson, 37–39. Ottawa: *Indian and Northern Affairs,* June 2006. https://publications.gc.ca/collections/collection_2010/ainc-inac/R3-82-2008-eng.pdf.

Campbell, Alastair. *Sovereignty and Citizenship: Inuit and Canada 1670–2012.* Ottawa: Inuit Tapiriiit Kanatami, 2013.

Crnkowvic, Mary, ed. *Gossip: A Spoken History of Women in the North.* Ottawa: Canadian Arctic Resources Committee, 1990.

de Coccola, Raymond. *The Incredible Eskimo: Life among the Barren Land Eskimo.* Surrey: Hancock House Publishers Ltd., 1986.

Dewar, Patricia. "You Had To Be There." *Inuit Art Quarterly*, vol. 9, no. 1 (Spring 1994): 20–29.

Diubaldo, Richard J. *A Historical Overview of Government-Inuit Relations, 1900–1980s.* Montreal: Concordia University, 1992. https://publications.gc.ca/collections/collection_2017/aanc-inac/R5-407-1985-eng.pdf.

Dorais, Louis-Jacques. *The Language of the Inuit.* Montreal: McGill-Queen's University Press, 2010.

Downes, Prentice G. *Sleeping Island: The Story of One Man's Travels in the Great Barren Lands of the Canadian North.* Saskatoon: Western Producer Prairie Books, 1943.

Ekho, Naqi, and Uqsuralik Ottokie. *Childrearing practices.* Interviewing Elders series, vol. 3. Edited by Jean Briggs. Iqaluit: Nunavut Arctic College, 2000. http://traditional-knowledge.ca/english/pdf/Childrearing-Practices-E.pdf.

Ejesiak, Kirt. "An Arctic Inuit Union: A Case of the Inuit of Canada, Greenland, United States and Russia." In *Nilliajut: Inuit Perspectives on Security, Patriotism and Sovereignty.* Ottawa: Inuit Tapiriit Kanatami, 2013.

Gaul, Ashleigh. "Between the lines." *Up Here*, September 2014. https://upheremagazine.tumblr.com/post/97578498738/between-the-lines.

Grammond, Sébastien. *Identity Captured by Law: Membership in Canada's Indigenous Peoples and Linguistic Minorities.* Montreal: McGill-Queen's University Press, 2009.

Greenwald, Barry, dir. *Experimental Eskimos.* Toronto, ON: White Pine Pictures and Paunna Productions, 2009.

Grygrier, Pat Sandiford. *A Long Way from Home: The Tuberculosis Epidemic among the Inuit.* Montreal: McGill-Queen's University Press, 1997.

Idlout, Lucie. "E5-770 My Mother's Name." *E5-770 My Mother's Name.* 2003. Youtube Video. Posted November 25, 2008. https://www .youtube.com/watch?v=LyCun8Le3jg.

Laugrand, Frederic, Jarich Oosten, and David Serkoak. "'The Saddest Time of my Life': Relocating the Ahiarmiut from Ennadai Lake to Arviat (1950–1958)." *Polar Record,* vol. 46, no. 2 (2010): 113–35. doi:10.1017/S0032247409008390.

MacDonald, G. "'When the Caribou Failed': Ilia Tolstoy in the Barren Lands, 1928–1929." *Manitoba History,* no. 45 (Spring/Summer 2003). http://www.mhs.mb.ca/docs/mb_history/45/tolstoy.shtml.

Marcus, Alan Rudolph. *Relocating Eden: The Image and Politics of Inuit Exile in the Canadian Arctic.* Hanover NH: University Press of New England, 1995.

Milloy, John S. *A National Crime: the Canadian Government and the Residential School System 1879 to 1986.* Winnipeg: University of Manitoba Press, 1999.

Newman, Peter. *Merchant Princes.* Toronto: Penguin Books, 1991.

NTI (Nunavut Tunngavik Incorporated). *Tukisittiarniqsaujumaviit: A Plain Language Guide to the Nunavut Land Claims Agreement.* Iqaluit NU: NTI, 2004.

Nungak, Zebedee. 2000. "E9-1956." *Inuktitut Canada,* vol. 88 (2000), 33–37. https://www.itk.ca/wp-content/uploads/2001/05/2000-0088 -InuktitutMagazine-IUCANS-IULATN-EN.pdf.

Nungak, Zebedee. "The Decimation of Inuit Security." *Arctic Focus,* September 9, 2021. https://www.arcticfocus.org/stories/decimation -inuit-security/.

NWT Council. *Council Notes.* Yellowknife, 1941.

Okpik, Abraham. *We Call It Survival: The Life Story of Abraham Okpik.* Edited by Louis McComber. Iqaluit: Nunavut Arctic College, 2005.

Oosten, J. & F. Laugrand. *Interviewing Inuit Elders.* Iqaluit: Nunavut Arctic College, 1999.

Peter, Auju. "Inuit Use and Occupation." In *Nilliajut: Inuit Perspectives on Security, Patriotism and Sovereignty.* Edited by Scot Nickels, Karen Kelley, Carrie Grable, Martin Lougheed, and James Kuptana, 43–48. Ottawa: Inuit Tapiriit Kanatami, January 2013. http://www

.polarcom.gc.ca/uploads/2730_20130125-En-Nilliajut-InuitPerspecti
vesSecuritySovereigntyPatriotism.pdf.

Pfieff, Margo. "A Man of Principle." *Up Here*. March 2012. https://
margopfeiff.files.wordpress.com/2012/12/david-serkoak-profile
-uh.pdf.

Pigott, Peter. *From Far and Wide: A History of Canada's Arctic
Sovereignty*. Toronto: Dundurn Press, 2011.

QIA (Qikiqlani Inuit Association). *Qimmiliriniq: Inuit Sled Dogs in
Qikiqtaaluk*. Qikiqlani Truth Commission: Thematic Reports and
Special Studies 1950–1975. Iqaluit: Inhabit Media, 2014.

Roberts, A. Barry. *Eskimo Identification and Disc Numbers: A Brief
History*. Ottawa: Social Development Division, Indian and Northern
Affairs, 1975.

Ross, W. Gillies. 1976. "Canadian Sovereignty in the Arctic: The *Neptune*
Expedition of 1903–04." *Arctic Institute of North America*, vol. 29,
no. 2 (1976): 87–105.

Sandiford, Mark, dir. *Qallunaat!: Why White People are Funny*. Canada:
Beachwalker Films and National Film Board of Canada. 2006.
https://www.nfb.ca/film/qallunaat_why_white_people_are_funny/.

Simon, Mary. *Inuit: One Future—One Arctic*. Peterborough: The Cider
Press, 1996.

Simon, Mary. "Canadian Inuit: Where We Have Been and Where We Are
Going." *International Journal* 66, no. 4 (December 2011): 879–91.
https://doi.org/10.1177/002070201106600415.

Smith, Derek. "The Emergence of 'Eskimo Status': An Examination
of the Eskimo Disk List System and Social Consequences." In
Anthropology and Public Policy and Native Peoples in Canada.
Edited by James B Waldram and J. Dyck, 41–74. Montreal/
Kingston: McGill-Queens University Press, 1993.

Reference Re Eskimos. 1939 CanLII 22, [1939] SCR 104. Accessed
March 13, 2022. https://scc-csc.lexum.com/scc-csc/scc-csc/en/item
/8531/index.do.

Tester, Frank, and Peter Kulchyski. *Tammarniit (Mistakes): Inuit Relocation in the Eastern Arctic, 1939–63*. Vancouver: UBC Press, 1994.

Tester, Frank, and Peter Kulchyski. *Kiumajut (Talking Back): Game Management and Inuit Rights, 1900–70*. Vancouver: UBC, 2007.

United Nations. General Assembly. *Universal Declaration of Human Rights*, 1948. [S.l.: Published by the United Nations Office of Public Information] https://www.un.org/en/about-us/universal-declaration-of-human-rights.

Wilson, Kory. 2018. "Appendix B: Indian Act Timeline." In *Pulling Together: Foundations Guide*, 85–86. Victoria, BC: BCcampus, 2018. https://opentextbc.ca/indigenizationfoundations/back-matter/appendix-b-indian-act-timeline/.

Appendix 1

When a map of the Keewatin District in 1926 is enhanced from a map produced by the Department of the Interior & Natural Resources Intelligence Services, it shows only 1 RCMP post at Chesterfield Inlet, 6 HBC posts, and 3 HBC outposts.

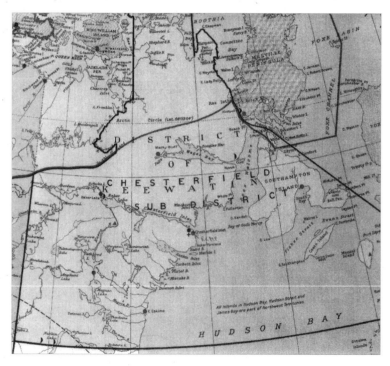

University of Alberta Libraries

Appendix 2

Keewatin District, 1929 shows 1 RCMP post at Chesterfield Inlet and a total of 13 HBC trading and outposts—the presence of non-Inuit in the area is increasing dramatically.

The Keewatin District in 1929, enhanced from map of NWT 1929, produced by the Department of the Interior & Natural Resources Intelligence Services.

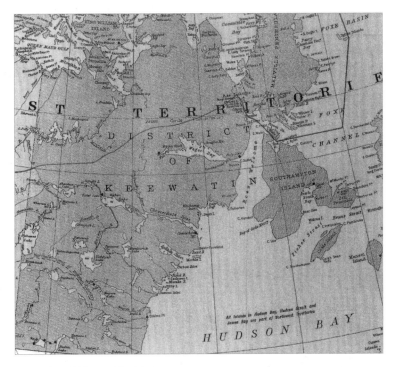

University of Alberta Libraries

Appendix 3

By 1939, two years prior to the launching of the Eskimo Identification Canada System, the Keewatin district now has 3 RCMP posts located at Baker Lake, Chesterfield Inlet, and Eskimo Point—within a decade, state presence has tripled.

Close-up view of Eskimo Registration Districts, 1939.

University of Alberta Libraries

Appendix 4

Eskimo Registration Districts are mapped in 1939, two years prior to the implementation of the Eskimo Identification Canada system.

Eskimo Registration Districts created by the Department of Mines & Resources, 1939.

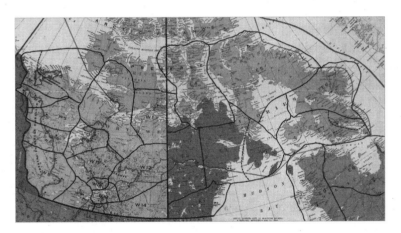

University of Alberta Libraries

Appendix 5

Birth of the Eskimo Identification Canada system by district map, 1945. Note districts W4–W14 are missing when compared to the 1939 Eskimo Registration map.

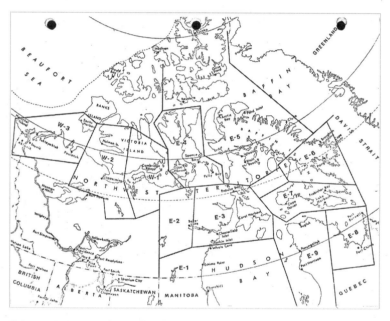

Roberts, A. Barry. *Eskimo Identification and Disc Numbers: A Brief History.*

Ottawa: Social Development Division, Indian and Northern Affairs, 1975.

Appendix 6

Appendix 7

Within seven sentences, the Eskimo Identification Discs issue pertaining to costs and appearance is solved.

(x) Eskimo identification discs   7717

        The Chairman referred to the increasing difficulty of identifying Eskimos and maintaining records of their hunting, education, hospitalization and relief because of the differences in spelling names. Dr. McGill said Indians were given a number and a check was kept of them at Treaty time but he realized this could not be done with Eskimos because there was no tribal system or Treaty payments. The Secretary reported that the field officers and missionaries had been consulted and no objection had been raised to the issue of numbered identification discs to Eskimos. Samples of Naval identification discs had been secured and were tabled for inspection by members of Council. The Secretary said that discs to be worn around the neck could be purchased for between $2.75 and $3.00 per thousand. Commissioner Wood remarked that this year would be the most appropriate time to introduce the system because an issue could be made when the census was being taken. The Chairman referred to the figure or likeness to be embossed on the disc and thought the Canadian Coat of Arms or perhaps His Majesty's likeness would be preferable. It was agreed that the Department of State should be consulted.

        It was then moved by Dr. McGill and seconded by Commissioner Wood that the system of identification discs for Eskimos be approved. Carried.

Appendix 8

AGENDA

One Hundred and Twenty-third Session
Northwest Territories Council,
Friday, 14th March, 1941,
11:30 a.m.

1. Acknowledgment from Mrs. Oscar
   Douglas Skelton — 9333

2. Appointment Hugh Llewellyn Keenleyside — 11942

3. Confirmation of Minutes -

   (i) One Hundred and Twenty-second Session,
   11th February, 1941 — 483
   (ii) Delete - "because drovers could purchase
   unhealthy cattle and dispose of the meat
   to the public" from explanation in No.
   4(i) - Amending legislation to control
   trading to benefit Indians — 483

4. Application of Province of Alberta for
   transfer part of N.W.T. — 6694

5. Development of Natural Resources -

   (i) Aids to prospecting — 11069

6. Northwest Game Act and Regulations -

   (i) Amending legislation to control
   trading to benefit Indians — 4017
   (ii) Closing Hudson's Bay Company posts — 2795

7. Radio (private commercial) - Application
   made by Hudson's Bay Company for stations at — 7802

   (i) Tuktuk (Fort Brabant)
   Rocher River
   Fort Liard

8. Migratory Birds Convention Act -

   (i) Enforcement by R.C.M. Police in
   N.W.T. and Yukon — 741

9. Mackenzie District Matters -

   (i) Aeroplane landing fields, N.W.T. — 8149
   (ii) Permits for consumption of beer in
   beer parlour, Yellowknife — 11092)
                                    563)
   (iii) Winter road from Rae to Mercury Gold
   Mines Limited property — 11933
   (iv) Territorial liquor profits account — 10651
   (v) Minutes Local Trustee Board, Yellowknife,
   30th January and 25th February, 1941 — 10710
   (vi) Consolidated Mining and Smelting
   Company — 4613

10. Agricultural possibilities Mackenzie District — 11858

11. Legislation -

    (i) Amendment to the Liquor Ordinance — 583

12. Employment of prisoners in N.W.T. — 9887

13. Arctic Matters -

    (i) "Nascopie" for Eastern Arctic Patrol 1941 — 5031
    (ii) Medical Officer for Eastern Arctic Patrol — 6276
    (iii) Medical student for Eastern Arctic Patrol — 5917
    (iv) Tourist traffic to the Arctic — 8135
    (v) Eskimo identification discs — 7717
    (vi) Louise A. Boyd Expedition 1941 — 5099

Appendix 9

Within 31 days of the previous 1941 session, the Northwest Territories Legislative Assembly, in two sentences, seals the fate of Eskimo identify for the next three decades.

```
(v)    Eskimo identification discs                          7717

              The Secretary referred to the discussion at the
last session of Council and reported that the Secretary of State
had pointed out that the likeness of The King or the Great Seal
of Canada could not be used on the proposed identification discs.
The Secretary of State saw no objection to the use of the Canadian
Coat-of-Arms.  The Commissioner, with the concurrence of Council,
ordered that a sufficient number of discs be struck bearing the
Canadian Coat-of-Arms to be distributed to all Eskimos in Canada.
```

NWT Archives/©GNWT/Legislative Assembly/G-1979-042-9-2 #2477

Index